Investigating History

The Twentieth Century

Acknowledgements

The author and publishers wish to acknowledge, with thanks, the following photographic sources:

Associated Press pp. 43; 44; 45
BBC Hulton Picture Library pp.8; 11 top; 11 bottom; 12; 27 top; 36; 48; 53 bottom
Bede Gallery, Jarrow pp. 20; 21; 22
Bridgeman Art Library p. 37
Camera Press p. 31
Historical Newspaper Service pp. 14; 46
Imperial War Museum p. 13
Photo Source pp. 35; 64; 75
Popperfoto pp. 15; 27 bottom; 28; 39; 46; 55; 58; 59; 60; 65; 67; 69; 72; 74; 76; 77
Punch p. 70
Stanley Gibbons p. 84
The Times Newspaper Group p. 73
Ullstein pp. 54. top; 56 top.

The publishers have made every effort to trace the copyright holders, but if they have inadvertently overlooked any they will be pleased to make the necessary arrangements at the first opportunity.

Investigating History

The Twentieth Century

M. V. Lyons
Head of Humanities Faculty,
John of Gaunt School, Trowbridge

MACMILLAN
EDUCATION

First published 1988

Published by
MACMILLAN EDUCATION LTD
Houndmills, Basingstoke, Hampshire RG21 2XS
and London
Companies and representatives
throughout the world

Text design Nigel Partridge
Cover design Michael Russell Design Associates

Printed in Hong Kong

British Library Cataloguing in Publication Data
Lyons, M. V.
The twentieth century.—— (Investigating
history).
1. History, Modern —— 20th century
I. Title   II. Series
909.82   D421
ISBN 0–333–39805–X

Contents

Preface

The great historian, Lord Acton, advised us to study problems rather than periods. Pupils are increasingly being presented with opportunities to investigate historical problems by using a wide variety of sources, as the emphasis in classrooms moves towards analysis, interpretation and evaluation of evidence.

This series aims to reflect the trend by posing a number of historical problems and by encouraging pupils to use the sources provided to investigate these issues. Each enquiry has been selected for its interest value as well as its importance in the particular historical context.

The books can be used in a variety of ways. Exercises may be used to enrich and to enliven the study of a topic or an issue. Alternatively the books can be used as the basis of a skills-based, concept-orientated programme which is diverse and self-contained. Each enquiry focuses upon a particular skill or skills and also upon key historical concepts.

Ideally pupils should have some understanding of the historical context against which each problem is set, but a brief background is included to set the scene. An introduction states the object of the enquiry so that pupils are made aware of the point of the exercise. At the end of each book is a summary grid showing the range of skills and competences pupils might develop in undertaking such investigations.

The intended audience for the series is pupils of eleven to sixteen years: it is expected that Volumes 1 and 2 will be introduced in the first three years of secondary school, while the third volume is intended for fourth and fifth year students, including GCSE candidates.

1 The sinking of the *Lusitania*

Introduction

You are about to investigate a historical mystery. There is no 'right' answer to this problem but your task is to use the evidence provided to support an opinion as to what happened and why it happened. At the end of the exercise you should also be able to give your views on these problems:

(a) What were the *consequences* (or results) of the event?
(b) Who *gained* most from the event?
(c) Why was the event so important *when considered against the background* of what was happening in Europe at that time?

Background

On 4 August 1914, Great Britain had declared war on Germany. It seemed to many people that Britain was the strongest naval power in the world but that Germany had the most effective army. At first the opposing sides were:

France		Germany
Russia	*against*	Austria-Hungary
Great Britain		Turkey (from September 1914)
Belgium		

Great Britain planned to use its great naval strength against the German navy. However, the Germans were not willing to risk large sea battles, knowing that their smaller navy might suffer heavy losses because they were outnumbered. Unable to force the Germans to a full-scale battle at sea, the Royal Navy was used to *blockade* the Germans. This means that British warships would prevent war supplies, such as food, ammunition, medical supplies, etc., from reaching their enemies.

By taking this action the British angered many countries who were not involved in the war. These were called 'neutral' countries. The Royal Navy stopped neutral ships, searched them and confiscated any war supplies (or *contraband*). German ships and those of their allies could be sunk. One neutral country which felt strongly about interference with its ships or people by either side was the United States of America. Britain was very eager for the USA to enter the war on its side but the Germans hoped that the USA would remain neutral. Neither side could afford to anger the Americans.

Countdown to Disaster

Cunard a passenger-ship company, probably the most famous in the world
U-boats German submarines

The *Lusitania* was *Cunard's* proudest ship, the fastest and largest passenger liner making the Atlantic voyage between the USA and Britain. Despite the fact that Germany and Great Britain were at war, many of the passengers were Americans who did not believe that a luxury passenger ship, even though it was British, could present a worthwhile target for *U-boats*. They thought that the German Emperor, the Kaiser, would not risk losing American goodwill by attacking a ship with American passengers.

One very important American who travelled on the *Lusitania* early in 1915 was Colonel House. He was the close friend and chief adviser of Woodrow Wilson, the President of the USA.

The dining room of the Lusitania, *one of the most luxurious ocean-going liners of the time*

Source 1

5 Feb. 1915 . . . This afternoon, as we approached the Irish coast, the American flag was raised. It created much excitement.

6 Feb. 1915 . . . Captain Dow had been greatly alarmed the night before . . . He expected to be torpedoed, and that was the reason for raising the American flag . . . The alarm of the Captain for the safety of his boat caused him to map out a complete programme for the saving of passengers, the launching of lifeboats, etc., etc. . . . if the boilers were not struck by torpedoes the boat could remain afloat for at least an hour, and in that time he would *endeavour* to save the passengers.

endeavour try

from Colonel House's diary whilst aboard the Lusitania (The Intimate Papers of Colonel House, *ed.* Charles Seymour, Benn, 1926)

Colonel House arrived safely in England along with the remaining passengers and crew on the *Lusitania*. Two months later the *Lusitania* was back in New York. The passengers who boarded the ship for this voyage would not be as lucky.

22 April A notice warning American travellers of the risks and dangers of the Atlantic voyage was published by the German Embassy. It appeared in newspapers on the morning the *Lusitania* was due to leave New York – 1 May (*see Source 2*).

27–30 April Four ships destroyed by German U-boats in the sea off Ireland near where the *Lusitania* was to pass.

30 April U-20 left the submarine base at Wilhelmshaven commanded by Senior Lieutenant Schwieger.

1 May Three merchant ships attacked by U-boats near the Scilly Isles. One was *Gulflight*, an American tanker. Three American lives were lost.
Lusitania sails from New York bound for Liverpool.

Ambassador representative of USA in Britain
prelude start

2 May US *Ambassador* to Britain, Mr Page, wrote in a letter: 'Peace? . . . Lord knows when! The blowing up of a liner with American passengers may be the *prelude*. I almost expect such a thing!'

3 May Another merchant steamship destroyed.

4 May German U-boat spotted off Fastnet (*see map*).

5 May A sailing vessel carrying supplies to Britain was torpedoed and sunk off the Old Head of Kinsale by U-20 (*see map*)

6 May Mr Page (in London) wrote in another letter to the USA: 'We all have the feeling here that more and more frightful things are about to happen.' U-20 sank two more steamships on their way to Liverpool.
Lusitania nears the coast of Ireland.

Was there sufficient warning?

Source 2

embark go aboard ship
zone of war area affected by the war
adjacent next to
formal notice serious warning

NOTICE!
TRAVELLERS intending to *embark* on the Atlantic voyage are reminded that a state of war exists between Germany and her allies and Great Britain and her allies; that the *zone of war* includes the waters *adjacent* to the British Isles; that in accordance with *formal notice* given by the Imperial German Government, vessels flying the flag of Great Britain or any of her allies are liable to destruction in those waters and that travellers sailing in the war zone on ships of Great Britain or her allies do so at their own risk.

IMPERIAL GERMAN EMBASSY
WASHINGTON DC, 22 APRIL 1915

from the New York Sun, *1 May 1915*

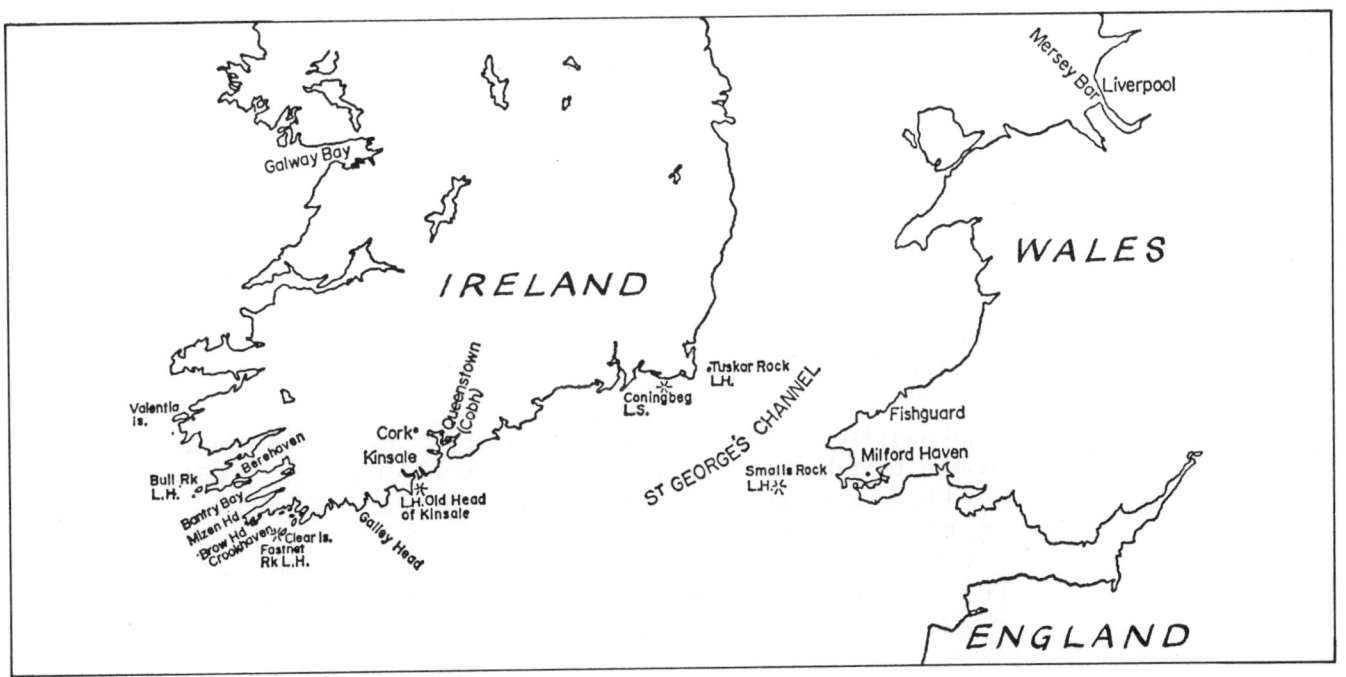

Source 3

headlands areas of land jutting out into the sea

6 May 7.50 p.m. Submarines active off the south coast of Ireland. . . .
8.30 p.m. Avoid *headlands*. Pass harbours at full speed. Steer mid-channel course. Submarines off Fastnet (*see map*).

7 May 11.25 a.m. Submarines active in southern part of Irish channel.
Last heard of twenty miles south of Coningbeg (*see map*).
Make certain *Lusitania* gets this.
12.40 p.m. Submarines five miles south of Cape Clear, proceeding West when last sighted at 10.00 a.m.

Wireless messages sent from Royal Naval command to Lusitania, *6–7 May 1915*

Source 4

convoy group of ships grouped together and protected by warships
forecastle head forward, raised part of a ship
crow's nest lookout post on the mast of a ship
bridge raised, narrow platform on ship from which the Captain directs its operation

In spite of what ticket agents might have told passengers, there had never been any thought of a *convoy*. There were no patrols on the scene. As a precaution two lookouts had been stationed on the *forecastle head*, an extra man in the *crow's nest* and a man at either end of the *bridge*; they scanned the ocean, but saw nothing.

from The Road to War – America 1914–1917 *(Walter Millis, a historian, 1935)*

Questions

1   (a) According to Source 1, what trick did Captain Dow play to deceive the German submarines? Do you think it was fair to use such a trick?
    (b) What evidence is there in Source 1 that Captain Dow was truly worried about the U-boat threat?
2   Look at the events of 1 May 1915. How do you think Americans would react to these happenings?
3   (a) How many ships were attacked by U-boats in the seas around Britain between 27 April and 6 May?
    (b) What precautions would you expect the British to take, knowing that U-boats were so dangerous to merchant ships?
4   Do you think the *Lusitania's* Captain and her passengers received sufficient warning of submarine activity in British waters? Use sources 2, 3 and 4 to support your answer.

Disaster strikes!

The British Cunard company employed many seamen, and the *Lusitania* was commanded on this voyage not by Captain Dow (Source 1), but by Captain Turner. At 12.40 a.m. on 7 May, the *Lusitania* altered course to move nearer to the headlands off the Irish coast. Captain Turner wanted to work out his exact position.

Source 5

starboard right-hand side of a ship
detonation explosion

Shot (torpedo) hits *starboard* side right behind bridge. An unusually heavy *detonation* follows with a very strong explosion cloud . . . . Added to the explosion of the torpedoes there must have been a second explosion. (Boiler, coal or powder.)

from ship's log – U-20. Recorded by Senior Lieutenant Schwieger, 7 May

Source 6

port left-hand side of a ship

On the Friday afternoon at about two o'clock we were off the southwest coast of Ireland, the Old Head of Kinsale (*see map*) was visible in the distance; my father and I had just come out of the dining room after lunching and were strolling into the lift on 'D' deck . . . . There was a dull, thud-like, not very loud but unmistakable explosion. It seemed to come from a little below us and about the middle of the vessel on the *port* side, that was the side towards the land.

from This Was My World *(Viscountess Rhondda, a passenger on the* Lusitania, *published in 1935)*

The sinking of the Lusitania – this picture was drawn by Charles Dixon from information supplied by survivors

Some of the victims of the disaster were buried in a mass grave in Queenstown, Ireland. Can you imagine how British newspapers reported such scenes?

Source 7

The people on the bridge just had time to see the track (of the torpedo) when they felt the shock and the crash of the explosion . . . . followed after a moment's interval (according to the overwhelming evidence of the survivors) by a second detonation. It seemed to have quite a different sound from that made by the

testified gave evidence as a
  witness
internal inside the ship

torpedo; 'It may possibly', as Captain Turner afterwards *testified*, 'have been *internal*'.

From The Road to War – America 1914–1917 *(Walter Millis, a historian, 1935)*

Source 8

wake track left by torpedo
  in water
Hunnish Pirates German
  pirates
wilful murder planned and
  deliberate killing

On 7th May, an uneventful voyage, the Irish coast was sighted and at 2.10 p.m. the liner was within 8 to 10 miles of the Old Head of Kinsale *(see map)*. Without the slightest warning, the *wake* of a torpedo from a German submarine was seen approaching the ship, and she was struck between the third and fourth funnels. There was evidence that a second, and perhaps a third, torpedo was fired, and the great ship sank within 20 minutes . . . . Men, women and children, caught like rats in a trap, were vainly fighting for their lives amongst wreckage of every description. The doomed liner's S.O.S. was answered within a few hours of the call, and 764 lives were saved. Still the *Hunnish pirates* had performed their task . . . . the foulest act of *wilful murder* ever committed on the high seas.

from the official version of the sinking published by the Cunard Company in October 1915. (Quoted in Lusitania *by Colin Simpson)*

A German view of the sinking – Admiral von Tirpitz with national flag fluttering proudly behind him above a picture of the doomed liner. The caption reads: 'Queenstown, 7 May 1915. The Cunard liner Lusitania is torpedoed and sunk.'

Reaction to the sinking of the *Lusitania*

Source 9

British poster on the sinking of the Lusitania – *the sword of justice is offered to America*

TAKE UP THE SWORD OF JUSTICE

A British propaganda poster – to whom do you think the invitation is addressed?

Source 10

From The Evening Mail *newspaper – New York, 8 May 1915*

An American newspaper reports the disaster.

List of Starters and Map of Route of Evening Mail Marathon To-Day on Page 13

HOME EDITION

WEATHER—Fair to-night and Sunday; warmer.

THE EVENING MAIL

79TH YEAR. NO. 109. NEW YORK, SATURDAY, MAY 8, 1915. ONE CENT.

HOME EDITION

WEATHER—Fair to-night and Sunday; warmer.

LUSITANIA DEAD 1502: 60 AMERICANS PERISH

1,300 RUNNERS AWAIT START IN MARATHON OF EVENING MAIL

Crack Long Distancers of Country Race Down Fifth Avenue and Broadway to City Hall This Afternoon to Cheers of Vast Crowds That Will Line 13-Mile Course.

KOLEHMAINEN SEEKS TO CAPTURE AMERICA'S CLASSIC A THIRD TIME

By FRANCIS.

Promptly at 1.30 o'clock this afternoon Justice Bartow S. Weeks will fire the shot that will start all of 1,300 conditioned athletes, the pick of the country, in the fifth revival of The Evening Mail Modified Marathon, under the auspices of the A. A. U., for scores of handsome prizes.

Great crowds, as in the four previous events that have gone into history, will line the course from the start, at 184th street and the Concourse, through the principal thoroughfares of the city, to the city hall plaza. A million people saw Hannes Kolehmainen race away to a brilliant victory over a select field last year.

The best police protection ever giver to the marathon runners will be provided. Commissioner Woods and Chief Inspector Schmittberger will direct the hundreds of policemen who will control the crowds and hold the line open for the runners.

FINISH POINT TO BE ROPED OFF.

Inspector Wakefield will rope off city hall, because the biggest section of the assemblage that will turn out to see the race there will endeavor to get a glimpse of the winner and those that follow in his immediate wake. Among the spectators at the "tape" will be Acting Mayor McAneny, Admiral Fletcher and officers of the fleet that steamed into the North river early to-day, and several hundred other persons of prominence.

As early as 11 o'clock some of the competitors will crowd into the public school at 184th street and Jerome avenue to don their togs for the 13 miles and 200 yards race. Checkers and clerks will be at hand to attend to their wants. Doctors will also be there to look over some of the contestants. Upon re-examination they can eliminate any young men they wish. Plans have been adopted to watch the runners, a secret service squad being on the lookout all the way to spot those that attempt to cut the course.

After the start the runners will proceed down the Concourse to 167th street, where a sharp turn will take them into Jerome avenue, continuing along that wide thoroughfare to Macombs Dam bridge, crossing the

CONTINUED ON THIRD PAGE.

REPORT A. G. VANDERBILT AND FROHMAN PERISHED

Theatrical Manager Missing Since Torpedoed Liner Sank—Cannot Be Found Among Survivors at Queenstown.

Survivors at Several Points Declare Vanderbilt Drowned—Some Reports Declare He Has Been Saved.

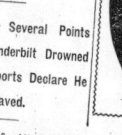

A. G. VANDERBILT.

London, May 8.—Alfred Gwynne Vanderbilt apparently perished wh[en] the Lusitania went down, according to a message to Ambassador Pa[ge] from the U. S. consul at Queenstown.

The "Times'" Queenstown correspondent says some of the s[urvivors] there report Alfred G. Vanderbilt was drowned.

CORK HEARS DEATH REPORT.

Cork, May 8.—It is reported here that Alfred Gwynne Vanderbit, o[f] New York, was one of those lost when the Lusitania went down.

FROHMAN MISSING, TOO.

Queenstown, May 8.—Every effort to find Alfred Gwynne Vanderbil[t] and Charles Frohman among the survivors of the Lusitania, landed here, has failed.

Wilson Walks Alone in Rain to Consider Action

Washington, May 8.—Profoundly affected by the news that great loss of life followed the torpedoing of the Lusitania, President Wilson and other government officials waited to learn how many American were among the victims.

In view of the warning from the United States to Germany that the latter nation would be held to a "strict accountability" for any loss of American lives, whether aboard neutral or belligerent craft, the eyes of officials and diplomats were turned toward the White House, where rests the final decision on the policy to be pursued.

Everywhere it was admitted that a grave international situation had arisen, whatever the number of American lives lost.

President Wilson and Secretary Bryan, it was believed, would make no announcements of policy until an investigation had been completed and all necessary facts concerning the incidents had been gathered.

President Seemed Stunned.

President Wilson seemed stunned when a cablegram received by the State department early last evening from Wesley Frost, American counsel at Queenstown, asked whether he should cable a list of the American survivors. An affirmative answer was sent.

Earlier messages received by the President had indicated no passengers had ben lost.

Within a few minutes secret service men on guard at the offices were surprised when a policeman, who guards the main door at the White House, rushed in and told them the President had just left the house unaccompanied.

Oblivious to Newsboys' Cries.

The secret service men rushed out in time to see the President cross Pennsylvania avenue and walk north through Sixteenth street, apparently oblivious to the drizzle which was falling, and to the newsboys who were shouting: "Extra, extra; many lives lost on the Lusitania. Americans among the dead!"

GERMANY REPEATS TORPEDO WARNING

The advertisement issue by the German embassy on the day before the Lusitania sailed from New York was reprinted again to-day in New York papers in the advertising columns. It warns Americans of the danger in embarking in British-owned ships.

Simultaneous with the appearance of the warning "ad" the Cunard line renewed its list of sailing dates for their ships, with the Lusitania stricken off. The first to sail from here will be the Orduna, on May 18.

Only 658 Known Survivors; Report 51 Americans Saved

London, May 8.—Fifteen hundred and two persons, including sixty Americans, lost their lives when the Cunard liner Lusitania was torpedoed and sunk off Old Head Kinsale, Ireland, according to an estimate by the British Admiralty to-day.

The known survivors number only 658 of the total ship's company of 2,160. The United States consul at Queenstown reports only fifty-one Americans are known to have been saved.

The list of Americans saved does not include the names of Alfred Gwynne Vanderbilt, Charles Frohman, Elbert Hubbard, Justus Miles Forman or Charles Klein.

Statements by survivors agree that the Lusitania was torpedoed without warning at about 2 o'clock in the afternoon, while a majority of the first and second cabin passengers were at luncheon. Some survivors said the liner sank within fifteen minutes after being struck, and others she remained afloat thirty minutes.

All agree that at least two torpedoes hit the liner. One struck near the bow on the port side and the other amidships, piercing the engine rooms.

FEW SALOON PASSENGERS SAVED.

Officials say the work of compilin gfigures of lost and saved is progressing slowly, but from all indications few first cabi npassengers were saved. The loss of life among the crew is also said to have been heavy. Capt. Turner went down with his ship, but was reported picked up three hours later.

Of the rescue fleet of torpedo boats, tugs and trawlers which went out from Queenstown, all but one have reported, and there is but slight hope that additional survivors will be picked up by fishing boats.

Of the survivors 595 were landed at Queenstown, 11 at Kinsale and 52 others are reported aboard a steamer.

The bodies of forty-five persons who died of injuries or were drowned have been landed at Queenstown, five other bodies at Kinsale and it is reported that the steam trawler Heron has picked up 100 bodies.

BODIES ARRIVING ON EVERY BOAT.

Later messages from Queenstown state additional bodies are arriving on every incoming boat. The Cunard warehouse there, used as a temporary morgue, is already filled and bodies are being taken to the town hall, hotels and private houses.

The American consul at Queenstown in a telegram to the United States embassy here said he had cabled the State department at Washington a list containing the names of forty-three Americans who have been saved. The message adds:

> There may be another dozen Americans not in touch with me. I also believe that one tender load of survivors landed at Clonwkikty.
>
> The survivors will proceed at noon or later this afternoon. The total survivors at Queenstown number 634. About sixty-three corpses remain unidentified.

A considerable number of the survivors landed at Queenstown are reported suffering from injuries and exhaustion. These have been sent to hospitals, which are practically filled. The less seriously injured are being attended by physicians at hotels or private residences.

The bodies of two little children, found floating on

CONTINUED ON SECOND PAGE.

List of Passengers Reported as Saved

AMERICANS

This is the list of Americans saved, as cabled to-day by Consul Lauriat at Queenstown:

O. S. Grab.
N. N. Allen.
Mr. Byington.
Mr. Brooks.
J. H. Brooks.
Clinton Bernard.
Owen Cannon.
Ed M. Collis.
Mrs. William Doherty and infant.
F. J. Gaunlett.
Duright C. Harris.
Charles C. Hardwick.
Oaden H. Hammond.
C. T. Hill.
J. H. Houghton.
Mrs. Nina Holland.
Charles T. Jeffry.
Fred S. Judson.
Robert Kay.
S. N. Knox.
George Kissler.
George A. Kessler.
Charles E. Lauriat.
James J. Leary.
L. B. Lines.
J. Linnson, Jr.
Herbert Light.
R. R. Lockhart.
Miss Loney.
Mrs. C. H. Lund.
Mrs. Thomas Mesh.
Dr. D. V. Moore.
William McMadams.
L. L. McMurray.
Patrick O'Donnell.
Stuart D. Pearl.
Ardray Pearl.
Major and Mrs. Pearl and two children.
Thomas Phillips.
Robert Rankin.
Mrs. Jessie Taft Smith.
Patrick Shattery.
Mrs. Stanley.
John M. Sweeney.
Arthur Shepperdson.
Thomas Slidell.
Edith Williams.
Mrs. John Wolfenden.
R. C. Wright.

ALL NATIONALITIES

Those reported saved are:

S. Abramowitz.
Mrs. Henry Adams, Boston.
Joseph Austin.
Julian de Aysla, Havana, Cuba.
John J. Balba.
Margaret Balbantyne.
H. Edgar, Birmingham.
O. Bernard, Boston.
Charles W. Bowing.
James Bohan, Toronto.
Miss Josephine Brandell, New York.
Mrs. Cyril H. Bretherton and two children, Los Angeles, Cal.
J. H. Brooks, New York.
Mrs. Burnside.
W. G. Burgess.
M. G. Byrne, New York.
M. Cairns.
Mr. and Mrs. Charles, of Toronto.
J. H. Charles and daughter, Toronto.
Guy Chambers.
Mrs. Davy Clamp.
A. R. Clarke.
Patrick Cliffe.
R. Colebrook.
Ernest Colloper.
Miss Conner.
Ernest Cowper, Toronto.
A. B. Cross.
Mrs. Cyrus Crosley.
Cyrus Crosley.
H. M. Daly.
Emily Davis.
Woodward Walter Dawson.
Dorothy Dodd.
Mrs. Doherty and infant.
E. A. Duckworth.
George Duguid.
R. Dyer.
John Ellis.
T. J. M. Evans.
Rovert J. Ewart.
Edward Fernandy.
Mrs. Fish and two children.
John Freeman.
R. Gardner.
F. J. Gautlett, New York.
Herbert Ghiberdot.
C. E. Gilhooly and child.
O. H. Grab.
J. P. Grey.
Rev. H. L. Gwyer and wife.
O. H. Hammond, New York.
Miss G. Hardy.
Charles C. Harnwick, New York.
Huntley Henderson.
Violet Henderson.
D. C. Harris.
John Herris.
Miss Holland.
A. L. Hopkins, New York.
J. Hooke.
Elsie Hook.
E. Housnell.
A. M. Jeffry.
Frances Jenkins.
Bertram Jenkins, New York.
First Officer Jones.
Miss Catherine Kaye.
George Kessler, wine importer at 20 Beaver street, New York.
G. B. Lane.
Mrs. H. B. Lassetter, of Sydney, Australia, wife of Gen. Lassetter.
Master P. Lassetter.
Charles E. Lauriat, Jr., Boston, Mass.
Percy Lawson.
Mr. and Mrs. Lewis and child.
Thomas D. Levin.
Joseph Levinson.
Second Officer Lewis.
Stanley Lines.
Miss Loney, New York.
Mrs. Andrew Lurdon and infant.
John W. McConnell, Memphis, Tenn.
Dr. McCready.
Jane McKean and child.
R. A. Mackenzie.
Lady Mackworth.

CONTINUED ON SECOND PAGE.

MACY'S ADVERTISEMENT APPEARS on page 7 of to-day's issue of this paper.—Adv.

GREAT BEAR SPRING WATER. 50c. the case of six glass-stoppered bottles.—Adv.

Leading Running Event in U. S. Sporting Circles.

The Evening Mail Modified Marathon is recognized as America's blue-ribbon race.

Thirteen hundred entries have been received.

The distance is 13 miles and 200 yards.

The race will start promptly at 1.30 o'clock from the Concourse and 184th street.

The finish will be in the city

The race last year was won by Hannes Kolehmainen, Irish-American A. C. His time was 1 hour 9 minutes and 1-5 second.

There is a time limit of 2 hours and 20 minutes. Athletes reaching city hall within that time will receive a survivor's medal.

Source 11

A medal produced by a German craftsman following the sinking of the Lusitania

Translation:
Side 1 (Below) 'The great steamer *Lusitania* sunk by a German submarine'.
(Above) 'No contraband'.

Side 2: 'Business before everything'.

Source 12

From our Department of State there must go to the Imperial (German) Government at Berlin a demand that the Germans shall no longer make war like savages drunk with blood.
from the New York Times, *8 May 1915*

Source 13

. . . Piracy, piracy on a vaster scale of murder than old-time pirates ever practised.
Theodore Roosevelt's reaction to the Lusitania *disaster (he was an ex-president of the United States)*

Source 14

decree of satan order of the devil
aloft above
sword of the Lord weapon of justice and truth

Truly the Nation of the black hand and bloody heart has got in its work . . . the *decree of satan* went forth from Berlin . . . . the Christian President of the United States, a cool and brave man . . . . should act, leaving no doubt that he is a leader of men and nations and that he holds *aloft* the *Sword of the Lord* . . . .
Marse Henry Watterson – American politician

Source 15

colossal huge
premeditated planned and deliberate

. . . it is a *colossal* sin against God and it is *premeditated* murder.
Rev. John Henry Jowett – US religious leader and politician

Source 16

forfeit lose
submit gives in

The United States must declare war (against Germany) or *forfeit* European respect . . . . If the United States came in, the moral and physical effect will be to bring peace quickly . . . . If the United States submit . . . she will have no voice or influence in settling the war or in what follows for a long time to come . . . .
Mr Page – US Ambassador to Britain

Questions

5   Compare the reports of sources 5–8 and source 10 regarding the number of explosions in the ship and what caused them. Explain the similarities and differences

in the reports.

6   What use was made by the British of the *Lusitania* disaster? Explain your answer with particular attention to sources 8 and 9.

7   According to sources 10 and 12–16, what was the reaction of some people in the USA?

8   What do you think the medal in Source 11 is trying to say? Which side does it seem to support?

9   According to the evidence provided, which country do you think gained most from the sinking of the *Lusitania*? Give reasons for your answer by referring to the sources.

Were the Germans justified in sinking the *Lusitania*?

The sinking of an unarmed passenger liner carrying many innocent passengers and having no warlike purpose is a crime which cannot be justified. The fact that there were many neutral American citizens on board seems to make the charge against the Germans even stronger.

However, it is necessary when investigating historical problems like this to ask questions – indeed to ask awkward questions, just like a detective who is trying to solve a mystery. Consider these questions:

● was the *Lusitania* unarmed?
● why did she sink so quickly?
● were all her passengers civilians?
● what was she carrying apart from passengers?
● did she get sufficient protection from the Royal Navy?

Now examine the sources that follow to see if these questions can shed new light on our investigations.

Source 17

Naval rifles high-powered naval guns

The reason why the crack liner *Lusitania* is so long delayed at Liverpool has been announced to be because her turbine engines are being completely replaced, but Cunard officials acknowledged to the *Tribune* correspondent today that the greyhound is being equipped with high power *naval rifles* in line with England's new policy of arming passenger boats.

from the New York Tribune, *19 June 1913 (The* Tribune *was a leading US newspaper)*

Source 18

fleet register list of fighting ships
auxiliary cruiser 'spare' or helping the regular fighting ships

By 8 August the *Aquitania* had had her guns installed and the *Lusitania* was moved into the Canada drydock on Merseyside (Liverpool) to be similarly equipped . . . . Her armament was installed and on 17 September she entered the Admiralty *fleet register* as an armed *auxiliary cruiser* . . . . The *Lusitania* was ready for war.

from Lusitania *(Colin Simpson, Penguin, 1974)*

Source 19

ingot brick-shape bar
shrapnel shell filled with bullets which scatter on bursting

– plans of cargo disposition and cross-section through ship.
Lower orlop hold (see plans opposite)
1639 *ingot* bars of copper spread over entire floor of bottom deck of ship.
Above these, 1248 cases of *shrapnel* – 3-inch shrapnel shells, filled, 4 per case.
3863 boxes of cheese ⎱   mysteriously addressed to a Royal Navy
696 tubs of butter   ⎰   experimental station.
600 cases canned goods.
329 cases of lard.
Several hundred packages of 'sundries' (i.e. various unknown articles).

Main orlop hold
76 cases brass rods
4927 boxes of cartridges – 1000 rounds of .303 ammunition per box.

Cross-section through the Lusitania

Position of the cargo on board the Lusitania when she sailed from New York on 1 May 1915.

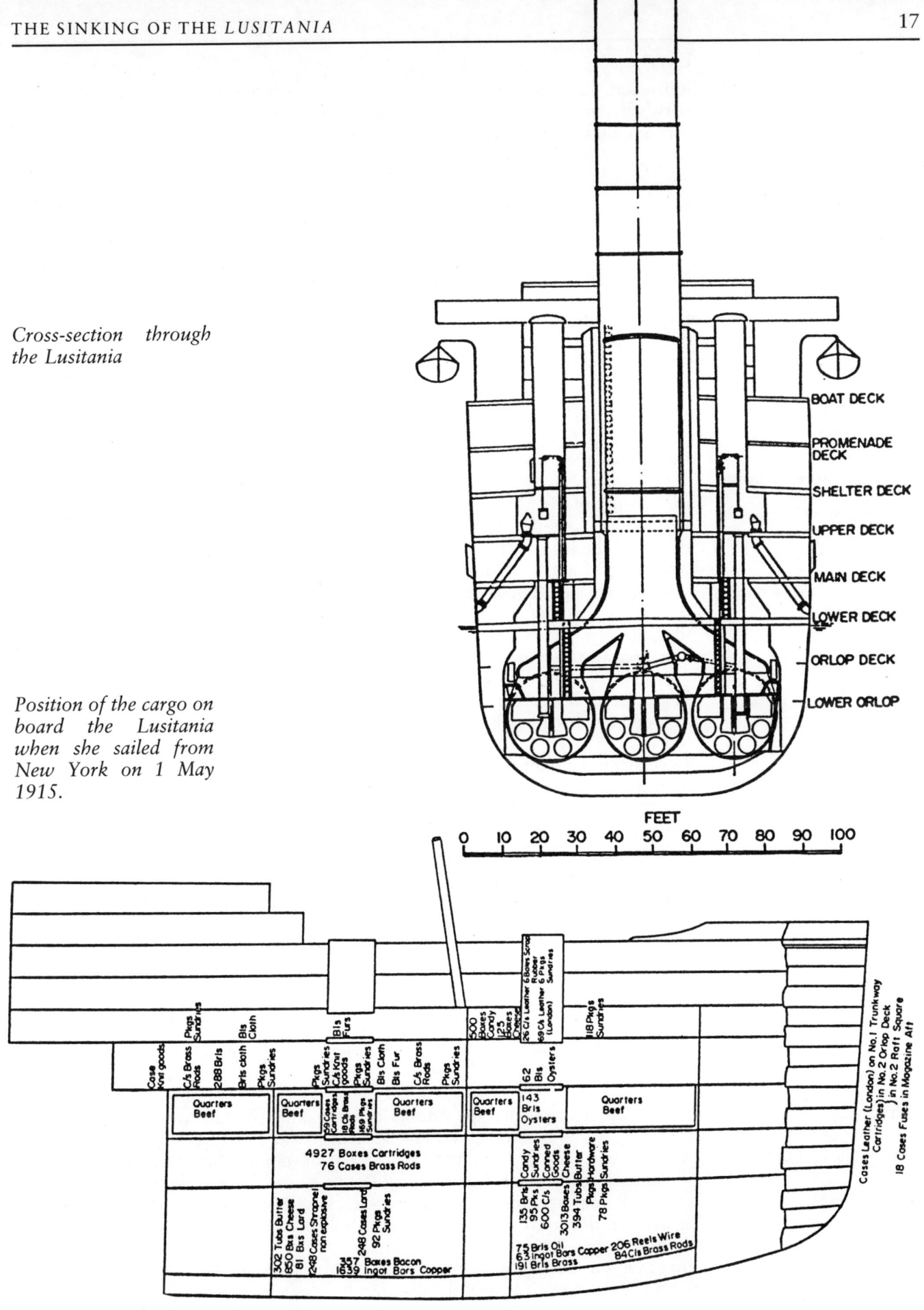

BOAT DECK
PROMENADE DECK
SHELTER DECK
UPPER DECK
MAIN DECK
LOWER DECK
ORLOP DECK
LOWER ORLOP

FEET
0 10 20 30 40 50 60 70 80 90 100

F Deck
Refrigerated compartment filled with sides of beef and barrels of oysters.
Forward part of the deck filled with undisclosed cargo – 'There is no doubt that it was ammunition'. (Colin Simpson, *Lusitania*, Penguin 1974)

E Deck
More brass rods.
62 barrels of oysters.
Sundries.
Cheese and lard for Cooperative Wholesale Society.
500 cases of candy (sweets).
323 bales of furs (Much evidence suggests that this may in fact have been 'gun cotton' – cotton used in the manufacture of explosives.)
Details of the cargo of the Lusitania *as it was loaded for its last voyage (Colin Simpson* Lusitania, *Penguin, 1974)*

Source 20

6th Winnipeg Rifles
   Canadian troops (Canada
   was Britain's ally)
draft detachment or group
   of troops, reinforcements

(On 30 April, 70 passengers were transferred, at short notice, from another Cunard ship to the *Lusitania*. Among them was a Mr Mathews, who later drowned as the *Lusitania* went down.)

The identity of Mr Mathews and his volunteers may be reasonably assumed from the report of a body washed up on the rocks of the Old Head Of Kinsale on 8 May, and the list of effects which were found on it: 'Male body identified as Lt (temporary)/Capt. R. Mathews of *6th Winnipeg Rifles* by certificates and papers found in his pockets.' The papers included steamer warrants (i.e. tickets) for himself, his two dependants (wife and child) and a *draft* of volunteers from the 6th Rifles.
from Lusitania *(Colin Simpson, Penguin, 1974)*

Source 21

Advice from W. J. Bryan, Secretary of State in Wilson's government.
'England has been using our citizens to protect her ammunition.'
and
'Germany has a right to prevent contraband going to the Allies and a ship carrying contraband should not rely upon passengers to protect her from attack.'
from Woodrow Wilson – Life and Letters *(R. Stannard Baker, Heinemann, 1935)*

Source 22

indignation anger

We spoke of the probability of an ocean liner being sunk and I told him if this were done, a flame of *indignation* would sweep across America which would in itself probably carry us into the war . . .
   (An hour later the two men were with King George V at Buckingham Palace.) We fell to talking, strangely enough, of the probability of Germany sinking a trans-Atlantic liner . . . . He said, 'Suppose they should sink the *Lusitania* with American passengers on board? . . .
Colonel House in his diary on a conversation with the British Foreign Secretary, Sir Edward Grey on the morning of 7 May 1915 (Charles Seymour, ed. The Intimate Papers of Colonel House, Benn, 1926)

Source 23

flotilla group of destroyers

(i) . . . the signs were that the Admiralty was taking steps to cover the *Lusitania*'s approach. Admiral Hood aboard the ancient cruiser *Juno* was steaming just south of the Fastnet rock and about to enter his patrol station where he was to meet her.
(ii) Admiral Oliver drew to Churchill's attention the fact that the *Juno* was unsuitable for exposure to submarine attack without escort, and suggested that elements of the destroyer *flotilla* from Milford Haven (*see map*) should be sent to her assistance.
(iii) . . . it was here (the Admiralty in London) that the decision was taken that was to be the direct cause of the disaster. No one alive today knows who took it,

but Churchill and Fisher must share the responsibility. Shortly after noon on 5 May the Admiralty signalled the *Juno* to abandon her escort mission and return to Queenstown (*see map*) . . . The *Lusitania* was not informed that she was now alone.

from Lusitania *(Colin Simpson, Penguin, 1974)*

Source 24

. . . it is a war against all nations. American ships have been sunk, American lives taken, in ways which it has stirred us very deeply to learn of, but the ships and people of other neutral and friendly nations have been sunk . . . . in the same way. I advise that the Congress declare the recent course of the Imperial German Government to be in fact nothing less than war against the Government and people of the United States . . . . We enter this war only where we are clearly forced into it because there are no other means of defending our rights . . . .

from President Wilson's speech to the US Congress 2 April 1917, in which he called for a declaration of war against Germany

Questions

10 Consider again the five questions on pages 15–16. In each case give your theory in response to the question and use any of the sources 17–23 to justify your theory. (You may wish to do this in the form of a chart.)

11 Bearing in mind your theories above, do you think the Germans were justified in sinking the *Lusitania*? Explain your answer.

12 Use the evidence provided in sources 17–23 to make either:
(i) A German newspaper report of the sinking of the *Lusitania*; *or*
(ii) A German propaganda poster justifying the sinking of the liner.
In each case remember to support accusations or ideas with the facts as the Germans might have seen them.

13 (a) Was the USA's declaration of war against Germany an *immediate* result of the sinking of the *Lusitania*? (Source 24)
(b) What phrases in the declaration of war indicate that German submarine activities were an important factor in American entry into the war?

2 The Jarrow Crusade
A study of motives and causes

Introduction

You may at some time have seen on television or read in a newspaper the story of a criminal trial. During the course of the trial the prosecutor must try to prove the guilt of the accused person. Before this can be clearly shown, the question of *motives* for the crime may be brought up. This means that the prosecutor tries to reveal that there was a reason, or perhaps more than one reason, for the accused person to commit the offence.

The question of motives, or personal reasons for taking a particular course of action, is not confined to criminal acts. We all have motives for acting in a particular way. For example, when we come to choose a job or career, we might have one or more of the following reasons:

money – the job is well-paid (*economic* motives)
status – we gain respect, admiration, a position in society (*social* motives)
power – it gives us control over others (*political* motives)
beliefs – we think that what we do is helpful or beneficial to others.

You may be able to think of other things which motivate people. An explorer or scientist might say that *curiosity*, a desire to find out, was his/her chief motive.

You are now going to examine the motives of a group of people, but at the same time you are also going to consider how things *outside their control* affected their actions.

Background

A bird's-eye view of Palmer's Shipbuilding and Iron Company in the 1890's. The works covered an area of about 100 acres. Try to imagine 100 football pitches!)

During the 1930s there was a great *depression* in world trade and industry. This had begun in the USA in 1929 and had spread to most other parts of the world whose economy was linked to American business and industry. Great Britain was particularly hard-hit. Even before 1928 this country had been losing in competition with foreign rivals such as the USA and Germany. The First World War had added to Britain's economic problems. When the American economy collapsed in 1929, the whole of Europe was affected.

The North of England was one of the areas worst-hit by the depression.

depression slump
crusade action planned to
support a cause

Unemployment became very high and the town of Jarrow in North-East England (*see map*) had one of the highest rates of unemployment in the country. In 1918 Palmer's shipyard, which was by far the main source of jobs in the town, had a work force of 10 000 people. In 1938 an official letter to Palmer's from London was returned with the message scrawled on in pencil, 'Not known. Gone away.'

Palmer's had been bought and closed down by the Government in 1936. That same year 200 men from Jarrow marched in a procession to London. This became known as 'the Jarrow *Crusade*'. The marchers aimed to present a petition to Parliament, and managed to reach London in 26 days, a distance of 291 miles from Jarrow.

The aims of this study are to try to reach some understanding of life and conditions in Jarrow after 1918 and to examine the reasons why unemployment rose so steeply. You will then attempt to work out the motives of the marchers, the organisers and supporters of the Jarrow Crusade.

Life and conditions in Jarrow, 1919–39

We may use a wide variety of evidence to investigate life and conditions in Jarrow between the two World Wars. One source which is particularly useful is the census which takes place every ten years. A good deal of the census information is kept secret until 100 years after the census is taken, but from the details that are released it is possible to gain a general picture of changes over the period 1921 to 1931.

Boom-time! The tragedy of the First World War did, at least, bring work to Jarrow. This picture shows the ships built by Palmer's during the war (1914–18).

Source 1

Employment in Jarrow in % from the census details of 1921 and 1931

Occupation	1921	1931
Agriculture	0.5	0
Mining	2.5	1.5
Metal works & Ship-fitters	30.0	11.5
Transport	5.0	2.5
Personal services	8.0	5.5
Commerce	4.0	5.5
Professions & Public Admin.	2.0	1.2
Craftsmen	6.0	4.0
Shipbuilders	5.0	11.0
Unemployed	35.0	52.5
Others	2.0	4.8

These figures tell us something of the changes that were taking place in the 1920s, but they give us little idea of life in Jarrow at that time. Throughout the 1920s Jarrow Public Health Committee reported annually on matters of public concern. From their reports we can build up a picture of Jarrow compared with other areas of the country.

Source 2

Death rates and infant mortality in Jarrow from Public Health Committee annual reports: 1919, 1931, 1936
Death rates per 1000 inhabitants:

	1919	1931	1936
Jarrow	20	15	15
National average	13	10	9

Infant mortality per 1000 births:

Jarrow	151	159	114
National average	58	62	57

Jarrow in 1932. Unemployed workers on the streets with time on their hands.

Source 3

dilapidated in ruins,
    decayed
pledged promised
bankrupt failed in business,
    collapsed

I returned home to Jarrow in 1921. There was no prospect of a job and the streets were becoming *dilapidated*. From 1922 I was unemployed. In 1929 I became a Jarrow Councillor and *pledged* myself to do whatever I could for Jarrow. Then in 1931 everything went *bankrupt*, and we in Jarrow had to suffer for it. Often my wife and I went without a meal on Sunday in order to feed the children. We patched up all our clothes as did all the others. In the town 156 shops were closed or empty. We pressed the council for more work and on one occasion I was thrown out of the offices during a meeting after saying that if nothing was done, then the riots taking place in Belfast would spread to Jarrow.

Joe Symonds, who later became Mayor of Jarrow

Source 4

pawnbroker one who
    loaned money but kept
    valuables as security until
    loan was repaid

The kids in Jarrow had no shoes at all. We set up a fund to buy shoes and we put a special mark on the sole so they couldn't be sold to the *pawnbroker*.

Mr J. Thompson, who became Mayor in 1936

Source 5

Statistics from a survey by the Jarrow Public Health committee
Occupation of houses in 1923

No. in family:	No. of families occupying no. of rooms:					
	1	2	3	4	5	6+
1–2	300	415	264	180	102	103
3–4	406	831	651	250	183	234
5–6	143	692	549	393	117	171
7–8	31	323	278	187	53	73
9–10	3	99	74	49	16	10
11–15	–	26	23	22	8	11

Source 6

We enter a tunnel-like passage with bare walls, and then go up a dark bare wooden staircase. At the top we enter the 'living' room of a two-roomed house. It is small room, perhaps 10 feet square. The room is crowded and hot. A fire burns in an old-fashioned grate. The washing hangs in a string, mostly children's garments, old and ragged. There is a broken-down sofa, a wooden table, two old plain chairs and cot . . . . A family of seven lives here.

from minutes of Jarrow Public Health Committee, 1933

Source 7

vermin rats, mice, lice, etc.
revulsion horror

The women polished their steps and the pavement in front of the steps was scrubbed. The backyard was washed regularly. Now that was it. The women had a hard way of life. There was a question of pride. Anyway they had to keep them clean or they would be overrun with *vermin* . . . You used to see the rat-catchers regular as clockwork. They used to have a bag and they swung it around so that the rats didn't bite through it. Rats are treated with *revulsion* now, but then they were sort of neighbours.

from The Social History of Tyneside, *H. A. Mess*

Source 8

infestation swarming,
    over-running

Complaints of *infestation* of premises by rats have been more numerous than in recent years. This year over 400 visits were paid by the sanitary inspectors. At one shop about 100 rats were killed.

Annual Report of the Medical Officer of Health, 1934

Questions

1   (a) According to Source 1, which occupations suffered most in Jarrow between 1921 and 1931?
    (b) Which occupation do you think was most affected by the closing of Palmer's shipyard?
    (c) When the main employer in a town is forced to close down, which other parts of that town's economy are likely to be badly affected?

2   Unemployment and poverty led to very bad living conditions. According to Source 2, how did this affect health in Jarrow at the time?

3   (a) If you were a government official from London investigating living conditions in Jarrow in order to write a report for the Prime Minister, how useful would you find Sources 3–8?

(b) What other kinds of evidence might you try to obtain in order to reach accurate conclusions?

Wages, dole and prices

statistics tables of figures

The employment figures shown in Source 1 tell us that over half the working population of Jarrow was unemployed in 1931, but these *statistics* are only numbers on a page. If we are to make a worthwhile investigation of how things really were for unemployed people in Jarrow, we must work out their standard of living – that is, what they could and could not afford. You should bear in mind that the working population of the town (the number of people who were available to work) was about 12 500.

Source 9

Unemployment figures from registers taken in Jarrow

Year	Men	Women	Boys	Girls	Total
1929	2798	231	123	93	3245
1931	5877	255	330	141	6603
1933	6469	192	380	137	7178
1935	5153	141	499	260	6053
1936	3407	100	298	260	4065
1937	3094	115	283	292	3784

Source 10

s = symbol of a shilling under the 'old' currency. One shilling was twelve old pence. This has now been replaced by the 5p coin

Average earnings for certain jobs, according to Ministry of Labour estimates, 1936

Men (earnings per week)	£	s
Printing, motor & aircraft manufacture	4	1
Iron and steel manufacture	3	17
Transport	3	11
Building	3	4
Clothing trade	3	3
Coal mining	2	16

Women	£	s
Motor engineering	1	18
Transport	1	16
Clothing	1	13
Public services	1	6

Source 11

d = sign for pennies under the 'old' currency

Unemployment Benefit and Public Assistance
(*NB* An unemployed person received Unemployment Benefit for six months only. After this, he/she received Public Assistance, a much lower payment.)

Unemployment Benefit available for 6 months	£	s	d
Man and wife	1	4	0
Dependent children under 14	0	4	0

Public Assistance after 6 months	£	s	d
Man	0	12	6
Man and wife	1	3	0
First child	0	4	0
Subsequent children	0	3	0

The following prices and costs will help you to complete your investigations into standards of living.

Housing   Average rent (per week)   9s   6d
               Mortgage on £500   £3   7s   0d per month
                         on £750   £5   0s   0d per month
                         on £1000   £6   14s   0d per month

Food   (Prices per pound weight, November 1931)

Bread	1³/4d	Cheese	8d
Flour	1¹/4d	Sugar	2¹/2d
Rice	3d	Tea	10d
Biscuits	7d	Beef	7d
Butter	1s 2d	Carrots	1¹/2d
Margarine	6d	Potatoes	1d
Best bacon	1s 11d	Beer (pint)	4d
Eggs (dozen)	1s 10d	Whiskey (tot)	5d
Milk (pint)	3d		

Clothing   typical prices for 'ordinary people' – though prices would obviously vary greatly!)

Ladies' frocks	5s 11d to £1 10s 0d (for a reasonable dress)
Ladies' jumpers	2s to 10s
Ladies' nightdresses	2s to 5s
Ladies' stockings	10¹/2d to 3s
Ladies' coats	£1 10s 0d

Task

Below you will find examples of two Jarrow families. Work in pairs to draw up a budget for each family for a week, using the following headings to guide you:
  (a) Rent or mortgage
  (b) Food
  (c) Fuel
  (d) Clothes
  (e) Money left for entertainment (including tobacco and drink), savings for a holiday.
You must bear in mind that £1 = 20 shillings
                        1 shilling = 12 pennies
(A shilling was the same as our 5p, so 15 shillings would equal 75p.)

Family 1 Mr and Mrs J. Armstrong
Mr Armstrong is a shipfitter earning £3 15s. per week.
He, his wife and two children live in their own three-bedroom house which cost £500.

Family 2 Mr and Mrs R. Scott
Mr Scott has been unemployed for two months and his wife cannot find work. They have three children of 15, 13 and 9 years. Their eldest child has left school but has not yet obtained a job. The family lives in a two-bedroom rented house.

Working in pairs, take one family each. Once you have completed your budgets you should compare notes and discuss the differences between the apparent lifestyles of the families.

Question   4   From your findings, write a paragraph explaining why many people in Jarrow at this time would have felt very unhappy with their standard of living. You could do this in the form of a letter to the local MP or to a Town Councillor.

Why did the Jarrow March take place?

Source 12

hangover headache and
   illness after too much
   alcohol
dismally miserably
boom time of economic
   growth
alleged claimed

Like a *hangover* after a good night, the year 1921 opened *dismally* for Tyneside and for Palmer's shipowners, faced with increasing prices for new vessels, cancelled contracts, or had work on ships suspended. It was a year when the wages of workers were attacked. Wages in the shipyards, despite strikes, were reduced by 6 shillings a week. Engineering, coal and railway workers suffered similarly. When the coalminers came out on strike, the iron and steel industry was affected. The shortage of coke was used as the reason for closing the iron works at Jarrow .... The works remained closed through 1921 and 1922. In 1923 it was open for 3 months then closed till 1927. There was another spell of work in the *boom* of 1929, but after that they closed again .... In the early 1920s British steel was sold at £24 10s. 0d. per ton .... Smaller countries like Holland were able to secure, by competitive prices, orders for British vessels.

In 1930 the NATIONAL SHIPBUILDERS' SECURITY LTD was set up. This company bought up and scrapped one-third of the British shipbuilding industry in an *alleged* attempt to save yards from the economic collapse. NSS were able by the financial weakness of Palmers' to buy it up at scrap prices. Holders of the ordinary shares, such as the workmen, who in better days had invested their savings were left with worthless paper. Protests were made but nothing effective could be done unless the government was prepared to act.

from The Town that was Murdered, *by Ellen Wilkinson, Labour MP for Jarrow during the 1930s*

Source 13

Palmer's was not alone. There was not a company that did not see its profits dive. On the River Tyne 5 firms closed between 1918 and 1931. The disastrous drop in demand was only part of the cause. The other part was the sharp increase in foreign competition. Late in 1926, for example, Italy launched the three largest motor liners in the world. Holland won an order for 8 out of the 12 large oil tankers placed by the Anglo-Saxon Petroleum Co. Ltd. Japanese naval architects, trained on the Clyde and on the Tyne, were now helping to improve their country's performance.

from J. Dougan, The History of North Eastern Shipbuilding

Source 14

In 1936 after a lot of pressure it looked as if the Tory government would build a new four million pounds steelworks. Then they said the plans had to be approved by the British Iron and Steel Federation. The BISF gave its blessing on condition that other steel firms in the Northeast accepted it, but one would not go along. Then the idea came to have a march. It was discussed by the Council in front of a packed public gallery. All the unemployed used to go to council meetings for a laugh to see and hear all the arguments and scenes going on, well into the night. They had no money to do anything else. About 1200 volunteered to march and 200 were selected. The council were determined to make it a non-political event and we wrote to hundreds of Conservative and Labour parties and Co-op societies.

Sam Ronan, a council employee in 1936, giving his account of the March (Newcastle Central Library, in 1976)

Source 15

We planned and advertised the march for men to come along. 2000 volunteered. Many of the young men had never had a job since they left school till they joined the army at 22 or 23 years of age.

Joe Symonds recording his memories, again in 1976

The Jarrow marchers arrive in London. Pouring rain did not prevent their progress through Hyde Park.

Source 16

resolution a written statement condemning or criticising an action

fascist political right-wing extremists who would not accept the rights of all individuals in a country

A dozen men* have said to the Men of Jarrow, you shall work no more. What is Jarrow's reply? Shall we just sit down and pass a *resolution* against this? I am prepared to march 7000 men to the House of Commons and demand justice. The working-class people of this town must rise in their strength and demand something should be done in their interests . . . . You can do no more in Jarrow. We are going to show this government we are determined not to accept their *fascist* principles. I don't want 500 people, or 1000, I want every unemployed man that can, to march to London.

(*i.e. Government ministers)

from a speech made by Joe Symonds, published in the Shields Gazette

Ellen Wilkinson, Jarrow's fiery Labour MP, addressing the marchers in Hyde Park, 1 November 1936.

The hopes of Jarrow represented in this box containing a petition to Parliament with 11 000 signatures. (This was followed by another petition from Tyneside with a further 68 502 signatures.)

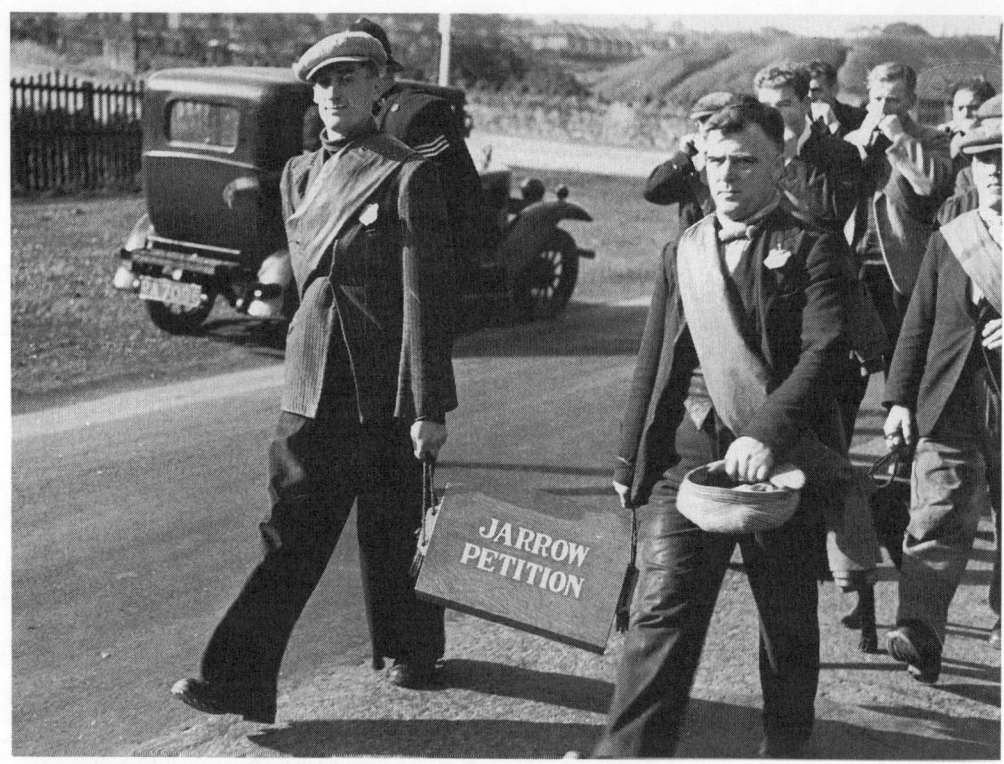

Source 17

A campaign was started by the Labour Party to send a petition. Then it was decided to march with the petition. I opposed the decision. There were hunger marches going on all over and I didn't want to embarrass and put down the men. I eventually had to agree, and I marched to Darlington with the men. I managed to get time off from Spillers in Newcastle . . . . Some Communists wanted to join us on the march, but we wouldn't let them.

Councillor Thompson, Mayor of Jarrow at the time of the March

Source 18

It was first of all intended to call it Jarrow Hunger March. I said that it was not a very nice name to have, and that the Jarrow Crusade would be a better title. And of course, we adopted the idea. At that time there was quite a number of marches being held all over the country, and they weren't being received too well in many places, although the reasons for their marches were no worse than ours.

David Riley (who was appointed a March marshal)

Questions

There was a drop in demand for ships throughout the world.	There was great competition from foreign shipbuilding companies.	British ships cost more to build than those of her competitors.
Palmer's shipyard was bought up and scrapped by the National Shipbuilders Security Ltd.	One North-East steel company objected to a plan to build large new steelworks in Jarrow.	There was a world economic depression.

5 (a) Examine carefully the grid above which shows a number of *causes* of the decline of Jarrow as an industrial, and especially as a shipbuilding centre. Now re-draw the grid, placing each cause *in the order in which you think it occurred* (i.e. if you think that world economic depression started the whole problem, then insert this in the top left square). You should use sources 12–14 to help you.

      (b) How much control could the people of Jarrow have exercised over these causes? Explain your answer.

6   The people of Jarrow may not all have understood world economic problems, or perhaps not even the difficult situation in which Britain found itself in the 1930s. What reasons would *they* give for their March in 1936?

7   Would you say that the *causes* shown in question 5 are linked with the *reasons* you have described above in question 6? Explain your answer.

8   What evidence is there in Sources 14 and 17 that the organisers of the March wanted to make it 'a non-political event'?

9   The Jarrow Crusade was a *protest* march. Can you think of any other ways in which people can and do show their anger at what they believe is wrong in Britain or the rest of the world?

10   Unemployment is again a problem in our country today. If you could interview someone who took part in the Jarrow Crusade and a person who is unemployed now, what kinds of questions would you wish to ask them in order to find out the differences between being out of work then and now? Make a list of these and work in pairs to interview one another. Try to work out answers by referring to the sources in this exercise and to your own awareness of the problems of unemployment at the present.

3 The destruction of Guernica

Introduction

Sometimes in studying history it may be difficult to understand why something happened. Events have occurred which seem, at first, to have had no reason or justification. Even when we do uncover some reasons, they may seem to us to be quite wrong or unnecessary. People do not always act as we would like them to and the pages of our history books are full of mistakes, tragedies, and even crimes which seem to have no real justification at all. You may be able to think of some examples from your own experiences in learning about history.

The object of this exercise is to investigate a great tragedy – the ruthless destruction of a small town in Northern Spain called Guernica. There is still argument as to who was responsible and why it was thought necessary to carry out such a savage attack.

Background

On 18 July 1936 a civil war broke out in Spain. A civil war occurs when different parties or groups in the same country fight one another for control. In this case the war was between two main groups. These were:

(a) *The Republicans* This was the side supporting the elected government of Spain. In general they believed in a state without a king, even though Spain had had a monarch for hundreds of years. They did not agree with the position of the Roman Catholic Church which had held tremendous power in Spain for centuries. Republicans also distrusted the strength and importance of the Spanish army. They wanted improvements in the lives of ordinary people though this might mean that more wealthy people might have to give up some of their privileges.

(b) *The Nationalists* This party believed in old, traditional Spanish ideas like the Catholic Church, the strength of the army and the importance of the more wealthy classes in the country. They hated the Republican ideas for changes, even though the Republicans had been elected to government by the Spanish people. Because they fought against the government, they were called rebels. Their leader was General Francisco Franco.

Before the war was many weeks old it had become a war of ideas as well as a civil war. It seemed to many Europeans that this was a war which showed how the whole of their continent was divided. In Germany and Italy, Nazis and Fascists supported the Spanish Nationalist rebels. In Russia, the Communist government gave its backing to the elected Republican government. Many individual people travelled to Spain from Britain, France, the USA and other countries, to join the so-called International Brigades to help the government forces.

The conflict in Spain had another aspect which is important to a real understanding of this investigation. In some parts of the country the inhabitants did not consider themselves to be part of Spain at all. These areas, particularly Catalonia in the south and the Basque region of the north-east, wanted independence from Spain. They did not recognise the Government in Madrid whether it was Nationalist, Republican, or any other form. They simply wanted to control their own affairs and to govern themselves.

The war was fought with a *ferocity* which shocked the world. There were mass executions, assassinations and murders. Nationalist tortured Republican, Republican tortured Nationalist. Towns and villages were bombed from the air and bombarded from the ground. Casualties were enormous and thousands became refugees after their homes were destroyed. Yet however horrifying all this was, few were prepared for the news that came out of the small Basque town of Guernica on 26 April 1937.

A map of Spain showing the advance of the Nationalists.

Guernica and its surroundings.

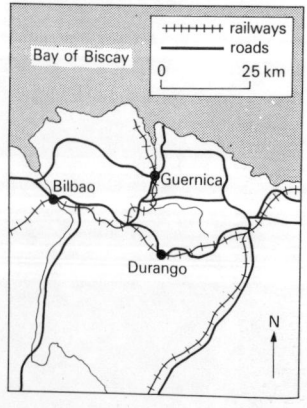

ferocity savagery, brutality

The accusations

Source 1

vilest most evil
affirm declare
alcalde mayor

As I stand before this microphone to tell the world what my eyes have seen in what was once Guernica, I call God to witness that I speak the absolute truth, which, in shame before the monstrous crime which they have committed, the rebels appeal to falsehood . . . . to deny the *vilest* deed known to history, the total and absolute destruction of the town of Guernica.

The wild beasts who piloted those aeroplanes, whenever they saw in the streets or outside the town a human figure, turned their machine-guns on it, sowing terror and death and killing not a few, among whom were women, children and old people. Such was the tragedy of Guernica, the truth of which I, Mayor of Guernica, *affirm* before the whole world.

It was not our militia who set fire to Guernica, and if the oath of a Christian and a Basque *alcalde* has any value, I swear before God and history that German aeroplanes bombed viciously and cruelly our beloved town of Guernica until they had wiped it from the earth.

from a speech by the Mayor of Guernica, 4 May 1937

Source 2

The truth was quite different, as I learned at the time from two journalist friends, an Englishman and a Frenchman, who entered the town with the first Nationalist troops on 29 April and closely questioned the inhabitants . . . . The Nationalists – not the German – air force did bomb Guernica, an important communications centre crowded at the time with troops, and hit the railway station and an arms factory. The burning and destruction of the town, however, were the work of Republican militiamen . . . .

from I Fought for Franco *by Peter Kemp*

Source 3

debris ruins

By 7 p.m. there was no Guernica. The planes had made a big killing. About a thousand men, women and children lay in pieces among the market goods, in the gutters, under the *debris* where their homes had been. The only things left standing were a church, a sacred tree (symbol of the Basque people), and just

The 'sacred oak' of Guernica – a symbol of Basque self-government. Behind it is the Basque parliament building.

outside the town a small munitions factory. There hadn't been a single anti-aircraft battery in the town. So easy had been the destruction of Guernica that the raiders came down to a hundred feet, and sprayed the survivors with machine-guns as they fled, terror-stricken, into the fields. Guernica never had a chance . . . . Steer and Holmes picked up some dud *incendiary bombs*. They were branded with the German eagle.

Noel Monks – one of the first newspaper reporters on the scene

incendiary bombs bombs designed to cause fire rather than just explosion

Source 4

military objective an important target for military reasons

Guernica was not a *military objective*. A factory producing war material lay outside the town and was untouched. So were two barracks some distance from the town. The town lay far behind the lines.

from The Times, *28 April 1937*

Source 5

Heinkel IIIs German bombers
Junkers 52s German bombers
Basque parliament house the building where representatives of the Basque people met to discuss their affairs
famous oak the tree sacred to the Basques as a symbol of their freedom

At half-past four in the afternoon, a single peal of church bells announced an air raid. There had been some raids in the area before, but Guernica had not been bombed. At twenty minutes to five, *Heinkel 111s* began to appear, first bombing the town and then machine-gunning its streets. The Heinkels were followed by . . . . *Junkers 52s*. People began to run from the town. These also were machine-gunned.

Incendiary bombs weighing up to 1000 lb, and also high explosives, were dropped by waves of aircraft arriving every twenty minutes until a quarter to eight. The centre of the town was then destroyed and burning. The *Basque parliament house* and the *famous oak*, lying away from the centre, nevertheless remained untouched. The number of persons killed has not been possible to establish. Estimates vary from 1600 to 100. The lower estimate is likely. But even the Nationalist commission of enquiry says over seventy per cent of the houses were totally destroyed, twenty per cent seriously damaged, and only ten per cent left moderately well off.

from The Spanish Civil War *by Hugh Thomas*

Source 6

A French anti-Fascist poster
Translation of message on poster: 'He who has done this is not with me but against me.'

Source 7

General Franco and the Nationalist rebels have now denied responsibility for the destruction of Guernica by bombing. They admit that Guernica has been bombed in the past, as a military target, but Nationalist Headquarters in Salamanca officially deny all knowledge of an attack on April 26. The Nationalists state that owing to fog no planes were operational on the Northern front that day. Foreign reporters are welcome to inspect log books and fuel records.

an announcement from Nationalist Headquarters at Salamanca

Source 8

contemptible worthless
atrocity reports reports of
mass murders, in this
case claimed to be false

George Steer's* flesh-creeping fairy tales of the alleged destruction of Guernica by German bombers are *contemptible* nonsense. What are we to think of serious, responsible newspaper like *The Times* when it allows itself to publish such tales? Nothing but the most evil kind of *atrocity reports*.

(*George Steer was a reporter from the British newspaper, *The Times*. See Source 3 in which his name is mentioned by Noel Monks.)

official German news report, 27 April 1937

Questions

1   In Sources 1 and 2 two different explanations are given of the way in which Guernica was destroyed. What are they?
2   Choose three phrases from Source 1 in which the language used by the Mayor expresses his bitterness at the people *he* blamed for the destruction of Guernica.
3   (a) Is there any evidence in Source 1 that the Mayor is a member of one side or the other in the Spanish war?
    (b) How might this affect the reliability of his evidence?
4   Peter Kemp (Source 2) claims that Nationalist planes bombed *military* targets only. How do Sources 2, 3, 4 and 5 agree or disagree about possible 'military targets', i.e. places with military uses or value?
5   Examine the *types* of evidence provided for you in Sources 1 – 8. There are newspaper extracts, eyewitness reports, official announcements, extracts from books and a poster. Which would you say were:
    (a) the most reliable (trustworthy) sources?
    (b) the most useful (informative) sources?
    Justify your answers.

The evidence used to support the accusations

Report from the Daily Herald, a British newspaper, 28 April 1937.

German Airmen Atrocity Shocks World

BRITAIN, FRANCE, SCANDINAVIA, THE UNITED STATES, ALL THE CIVILISED WORLD HEARD WITH HORROR YESTERDAY OF THE BOMBING OF MEN, WOMEN AND CHILDREN IN GUERNICA, ANCIENT CAPITAL OF THE LOYAL BASQUES.

German airmen, fighting for rebel General Franco and flying German bombing 'planes, swept down from a clear sky on the defenceless, peaceful town. They left it, three hours later, a town of death and fire, its little white houses ablaze, the narrow cobbled streets paved with dead and dying.

At least 800 people were killed; several thousands were wounded.

Fugitives were pursued into the fields by the airmen and shot down as they ran.

BLESSING AS BOMBS FELL

From A Special Correspondent
BILBAO, Tuesday.

AS bombs were rained by German airmen on Guernica, during the worst atrocity of the century, an elderly priest called his people into the market-place.

The people knelt before him, and he raised his hand to give them his blessing.

Source 9

aerial bombardment
    bombing from the air

The direct evidence that Guernica had been destroyed by *aerial bombardment* is as follows: the town and the roofs that were still unburnt were a mass of bomb holes. Trees were snapped off at the stem. Foliage was torn away by bomb splinters. Of these bomb splinters I collected several: they are of exactly the same metal as the bombs lately used by the Germans in the fighting. Of incendiary bombs I picked up three, all German, dated 1936. I was in Guernica until 1.30 a.m. on April 27th, but sniff where I might I could catch no odour of petrol. In any case, victims injured in the raid were not treated for petrol burns, but for bomb wounds. I myself, saw the bodies of 14 dead people: all but two of them were killed by bombs, and those two died by machine gun bullets.

from a report in The Times *by reporter George Steer, April 1937*

Source 10

laying waste destroying
incendiaries people who
    deliberately burn down
    buildings
cronies supporters

The Republicans' friends have blown up the city of Irun. They used dynamite and liberally sprayed petrol until most of the buildings were destroyed. At Madrid and Malaga and countless other Spanish towns, Republicans have demonstrated how skilful they are at blowing up buildings – and *laying waste* streets and houses. These *incendiaries* were at Guernica too: the destructions and the great fire and explosions which during one whole day occurred at Guernica were the work of the Republicans. For the news reports of the so-called air raid as published in British and other foreign newspapers are nothing but a slander campaign by the Communists and their *cronies*.

announcement from Nationalist headquarters at Salamanca, 4 May 1937

Source 11

arson deliberately setting
    fire to

There was an arms factory in Guernica, which produced trench mortars, pistols and other weapons. Our planes bombed this arms factory and also bombed the railway station to prevent the arms from being exported. When I went into Guernica on April 29th, the day the Nationalists captured the town, I saw two completely different kinds of ruins, on one side the bombed arms factory, the railway station and their surroundings, and on the other, ruins of a more recent character, the result of *arson* and dynamite.

the Nationalist General, Martinez España

Source 12
systematically deliberately

I saw the destruction at Irun which was certainly burnt on the ground by Republican forces. A complete street, the main street of Irun, was *systematically* destroyed house by house with only the walls left standing, and the interiors completely gutted by fire. A rain of bombs might also destroy a whole street in a town, but it would not destroy it in that way. At Guernica, as in Irun, there is hardly a mark in the street, the rain of bombs would fall as often in the streets and gardens as on the houses, and must leave traces which could not possibly be obliterated. A bomb falling from a height would tear its way through a house which the bomb hits would totally destroy, and the outside walls would never be left intact. But walls were left intact at Guernica.

an English publisher, Douglas Jerrold, who supported Franco (June 1937)

Source 13

. . . it is now in fact admitted that the bombers were in action 'intermittently over a period of three hours' . . . . Independent reports have also established beyond doubt that the aircraft involved in bombing and machine-gunning were of German make, and several unexploded incendiary bombs have been recovered bearing the stamp of a German factory. The identity and the nationality of the pilots are not yet known; but they can hardly remain a secret for long.

from The Times, *5 May 1937*

Source 14

It was Monday and market day. We were passing near the railroad station when we heard a bomb explosion; it was followed immediately by two others. An aeroplane which was flying very low dropped its load and left, all in a few seconds. It was Guernica's first war experience. The panic of the first moments shocked the inhabitants and the peasants come in to market. We observed a considerable excitement. We got out of the automobile and tried to find out what was happening and to calm the many women who were growing more nervous and excited. Minutes later other bombs fell near the Convent of the Madres Mercedarias and the people began to leave the streets and to hide in cellars and under shelters. There very soon appeared, as if coming from the sea, some eight heavy planes which dropped many bombs and behind them followed a *veritable* rain of incendiary bombs. For more than three hours there followed waves of bombers, of airplanes with incendiary bombs and of solitary machines which came down to two hundred metres to machine-gun the poor people who fled in fright.

veritable genuine, actual

Eye-witness report of Father Alberto de Onaindia, a visiting Catholic priest who was trying to locate his mother near Guernica. (He wrote this description some years after the attack.)

Source 15

pursuit plane fighter aircraft

His diary shows the word 'Guernica' on April 26, the day when the town was destroyed. Wandel admitted that Guernica had been bombed, but said that he, as pilot of a *pursuit plane*, did not take part. He had accompanied German bombers on other expeditions when they destroyed Basque pinewoods with incendiary bombs, which, he said, were highly efficient.

A report by George Steer of The Times *concerning a German pilot called Hans Wandel, shot down by government forces on 13 May 1937*

Source 16
Photograph showing the damage to the town of Guernica

Source 16
Photograph showing damage caused by incendiary bombs during the German blitz on London in later 1940

Source 17

The Nationalist Press Officer at Salamanca said that everyone knew that Guernica was not bombed by the Nationalists; it was burned by the Republicans and their Communist friends. He offered to drive me to Guernica so that I could see for myself . . . .

. . . Guernica was a lonely chaos of timber and brick. There were only three or four people in the streets; one old man was standing inside an apartment house that had four sides to it, but an interior that was only a sea of bricks. It was his job to clear away the debris. Accompanied by the Press Officer I went up to him and asked him if he had been in Guernica during the destruction in April. He nodded his head, and when I enquired what had happened, he waved his arms in the air and said that the sky had been black with German and Italian planes. 'Aeroplanes,' he said, 'Italian and German'. The Press Officer turned pale.

'Guernica was burned,' he contradicted. The old man stuck to his point, however. After a four-hour bombardment, he insisted, there was little left to burn. The Press Officer moved me away. 'Juan is a Communist,' he said. We talked to two more other people, who gave us the same story about the aeroplanes. The Press Officer lapsed into silence.

Later in the day we met two Nationalist officers and he brought the subject up. 'Guernica is full of Communists,' he complained. 'They tried to tell us it was bombed not burned.'

'Of course it was bombed,' said one of the officers. 'We bombed it and bombed it and bombed it. Why not?'

The Press Officer never spoke of Guernica again.

Sunday Times reporter at Nationalist HQ, Salamanca, October 1937

Source 18

Führer 'leader' – Adolf Hitler
AA guns anti-aircraft guns
rotation regular turnaround or change

Guernica – the famous picture by the Spanish artist Pablo Picasso, (1881–1973). What impression does this painting convey to you?

When civil war broke out in Spain, Franco sent an appeal for help to Germany, especially for support in the air. The *Führer* hesitated and I strongly urged him to give the support under any circumstances – first, to combat the spread of Communism in that region, but also to try out my young Air Force on a number of technical points. With the Führer's approval I despatched a large part of my transport fleet and a number of training units of my fighters and bombers, also some *AA guns*; in this way I had the opportunity of testing under fire whether the material had been developed in an efficient manner. So that the personnel should also acquire practical experience I arranged a steady *rotation*, repeatedly sending out new units and recalling others.

from the testimony of Hermann Göring (Commander of Nazi Germany's Air Force), at his trial in Nuremberg, 1945–6

Questions

6 Using Sources 9 and 15 to 17, explain in your own words the various pieces of evidence which indicate that Guernica was destroyed from the air and that German aircraft were involved.

7 From Sources 10, 11 and 12, explain the evidence used by the Nationalists and their supporters to blame the Republicans for the destruction of Guernica.

8 Source 6 seems to leave no doubt at all as to who was responsible.
   (a) What symbols indicate the cartoonist's disgust at the destruction of Guernica?
   (b) How does he show who he thinks was responsible?

9 Does the evidence of Göring (Source 18) help us at all? Explain your opinion.

10 The Republicans had shown before the Civil War that they would give self-government to Catalonia, one of the regions that wanted its independence from

Spain. The Nationalists, however, were determined to keep Spain together as one undivided nation. Do you think that this fact, if used with Sources 3 and 5, can help us decide who had most to gain from the destruction of Guernica?

11   Using all the evidence you have examined, write a paragraph to explain which side you think was responsible. Support your theory with references to the evidence.

4 The assassination of Trotsky

Introduction

History is about people and it is important that we sometimes give attention to the role of individuals in historical events and developments. One question we might usefully ask is, 'What was the contribution of a particular person to an historical event?' This is a very broad question because it leads us to others, such as:
- did he/she contribute to the *causes* of the events?
- did he/she influence the *course or development* of events?
- what were the *consequences* of his/her actions?

Perhaps you can think of some more.

In this exercise you will be investigating the role of one particular individual but, as you will see, his actions had a very dramatic effect on other individuals and events on the world stage.

Background

Timeline

banished sent away
eliminate kill or imprison
asylum protection

1917 October. Second revolution in Russia brought the Bolsheviks to power. Lenin and Trotsky were leading figures in the new Soviet State.

1918 Trotsky was Foreign Minister. Led the peace talks with the Germans which took Russia out of the First World War.

1918–21 Civil War in Russia between Bolsheviks (and their supporters) and their enemies. Trotsky led the new 'Red Army' to success over the Bolsheviks' foes.

1924 Lenin, leader of the new Soviet State, died.

1924–26 Struggle for the leadership of Russia brought Trotsky into open conflict with Stalin, his rival for power.

1928 Stalin took over supreme control of Russia. Trotsky, who opposed him, was *banished* to a remote part of the country.

1929 Trotsky was forced by Stalin into exile abroad.

Left to right, Stalin, Lenin and Trotsky. When Lenin died in 1924, the other two became deadly enemies.

1935 Stalin began his Purges – that is, he tried to *eliminate* anyone hostile to his actions or people he regarded as a threat to his power. In Norway Trotsky wrote *The Revolution Betrayed*, a book in which he attacked Stalin's actions.

1937 Trotsky settled in Mexico, the only country in the world prepared to offer him *asylum*.

The split between Trotsky and Stalin

Source 1

General Secretary (of the Communist Party)
Central Committee the small group of ministers who held most power in the Soviet Union

Since he became *General Secretary*, Comrade Stalin has taken into his hands immeasurable power, and I am not sure that he will always know how to use that power with sufficient care. On the other hand, Comrade Trotsky .... is marked out not only by his outstanding abilities. He is personally the most capable person in the present *Central Committee* but he suffers from too much self-confidence and is too liable to be carried away by the purely administrative side of a problem .... Comrade Stalin is too rude .... unacceptable in a General Secretary. That is why I suggest the comrades think about a way to remove Stalin from that post and appoint in his place another man who in all respects differs from Comrade Stalin .... that is, more tolerant, more loyal, more polite and more considerate of the comrades ....

from 'Letter to the Congress' by Lenin, late 1922

Source 2

Had I not been present in 1917 in Petrograd the October Revolution would still have taken place – on condition that Lenin was present and in command.

   If neither Lenin nor I had been present in Petrograd, there would have been no October Revolution ....

from Diary in Exile, *by Leon Trotsky*

Source 3

He (Stalin) is unhappy at not being able to convince everyone, himself included, that he is greater than everyone .... because of this unhappiness he cannot help taking revenge on people, on all people, but especially those who are in any way higher or better than he. If someone speaks better than he does, that man is doomed! Stalin will not let him live because that man is a constant reminder that he, Stalin, is not the first and the best. If someone writes better, matters are bad for him because he, Stalin, has to be the best Russian writer .... He is a small-minded, malicious man – no, not a man, but a devil.

An opinion of Stalin by another Bolshevik leader, Nikolai Bukharin, one of the leaders of the October 1917 revolution (later executed during Stalin's purges)

Source 4

cartoon of 1930 showing a circus of Stalin's enemies. (Trotsky is at the very front to the left of the weightlifter)

Source 5

slandered made untrue statements about

Stalin, you have started a new stage which will go down in the history of our revolution as the 'period of terror'. No one feels safe in the Soviet Union. No one, as he goes to bed, knows whether he will escape arrests in the night . . . . With the help of dirty forgeries you have staged trials . . . . You have *slandered* and shot old colleagues of Lenin knowing very well that they were innocent. You have forced them before dying to confess crimes they never committed, to cover themselves in filth from head to toe.

An extract from an open letter (one the public could read) to Stalin by Fyodor Raskolnikov, a Bolshevik hero who, for fear of Stalin's revenge, went into voluntary exile abroad

Source 6

dregs of humanity lowest of the low

In 1937 new facts came to light regarding the devilish crimes of the Bukharin–Trotsky gang . . . . The trials showed that these *dregs of humanity* . . . enemies of the people . . . . had been in conspiracy against Lenin, the (Communist) Party and the Soviet State ever since the early days of the October Revolution . . . . The trials brought to light the fact that the Trotsky–Bukharin devils, obeying the wishes of their masters – the spy services of foreign states – had set out to destroy the Party and the Soviet state . . . . The Soviet court sentenced the Bukharin – Trotsky devils to be shot . . . . *
(*Bukharin was executed in 1938.)

from Short History of the Communist Party of the Soviet Union, *1938*

An anti-Stalin poster showing how Lenin's former friends and advisers were eliminated. Was this printed before or after Trotsky's death?

Questions

1   What evidence is there in Source 1 that Lenin had realised by 1922 that Stalin was not a suitable choice as the General Secretary of the Communist Party in the Soviet Union?

2   (a) Both Bukharin (Source 3) and Raskolnikov (Source 5) were old friends of Lenin and heroes of the October 1917 revolution. Do you think this makes their judgement of Stalin easier to believe?
    (b) If Bukharin *is* to be believed, why did Stalin try to eliminate all his opponents?

3   Is Source 4 for or against Stalin? Explain your answer by referring to the cartoon.

4   (a) Do you think Lenin's view of Trotsky (Source 1), is supported by Trotsky's own claims in Source 2? Explain your answer.
    (b) If Lenin's view of Trotsky was correct and Trotsky's opinion of his own contribution to the October Revolution was accurate, what might Stalin feel about him?

Trotsky in exile

Some of the books Trotsky wrote whilst in exile:
The Stalin School of Falsification.
The Revolution Betrayed.
Stalin.
The Real Situation in Russia.

falsification lying

Source 7

'his myth might grow'
Trotsky might become a martyr and a symbol of resistance against Stalin
more savage precautions eliminate him

There is some mystery about why Stalin had allowed Trotsky out of Russian territory – why he did not have him imprisoned or killed . . . . But at the end of the 1920s it would have been dangerous for Stalin to try to destroy Trotsky – in this event *his myth might grow* and might turn to destroy Stalin. There was still an enormous power just in Trotsky's name, both in Russia and in Western Europe . . . . he (Stalin) could always keep an eye on Trotsky even outside Russia–and take *more savage precautions* when the moment came.

Stalin would not allow his most dangerous enemy to remain in the Soviet Union. Even when he sent Trotsky to remote, isolated parts of Russia, he could not be sure that the power of Trotsky's personality and the memory of his great contribution to the Revolution would not attract support.
from The Assassination of Trotsky *(Nicholas Mosley, Abacus, 1972)*

Timeline of exile
Feb 1929 Trotsky and family left for Turkey.
July 1933 Trotsky was granted permission to stay in France.
June 1935 Trotsky was expelled by the French Government and allowed to live in Norway.
Dec 1936 Trotsky was offered asylum in Mexico by President Cardenas.

Source 8

disgruntled veterans from Spain Communists who had fought on the losing side in the Spanish Civil War and followed Stalin
distraught members of the Mexican Communist Party Mexican Communists who disliked Trotsky's criticisms of Stalin

Trotsky knew that so long as President Cardenas stood firm about allowing him to remain in Mexico, then sooner or later an attempt on his life would be made . . . . The attempt would be made either by trained agents of Stalin's secret political police – the GPU – who were rumoured now to be arriving in force in Mexico City, by the *disgruntled veterans from Spain*, by *distraught members of the Mexican Communist Party*, or by some combination of all three.
from The Assassination of Trotsky *(Nicholas Mosley, Abacus, 1972)*

Source 9

dulled senses drowsiness
odour smell
acrid irritating; bitter and hot
villa house

At about four in the morning of 23 May 1940, Trotsky, after a hard day's work, nevertheless needed a sleeping pill, which he took after going to bed late. He was woken up by the sound of machine-gunfire, which, to his *dulled senses* sounded for a moment like the fireworks common on Mexican holidays. The next second it was plain what it was: 'the explosions were too close, right here within the room, next to me and overhead. The *odour* of gunpowder became more *acrid* . . . . we were under attack' . . . . Later an estimate of 100 shots was made, close to us on the beds. Seventy were noted in the walls and doors . . . . A few minutes after the gunfire had stopped, everyone in the *villa* rushed out into the courtyard. Nothing had happened; no one was hurt . . . .
from Trotsky *(Joel Carmichael, Hodder and Stoughton, 1975)*

Source 10

(Salazar asked Trotsky if he suspected anyone.)
'I most certainly do!' he replied in a very decided tone of voice. 'Come . . . ' He put his right hand on my shoulder and slowly led me towards the rabbit hutches . . . . He stopped, glanced all round him to make sure that we were alone, and, placing his right hand near his mouth, as though wishing to make the confidence more secret, he said in a low voice with deep *conviction*:

'The author of the attack is Joseph Stalin'.

from the Report of Colonel Salazar, head of the Mexican Secret Police

Questions

5   Bearing in mind Trotsky's great contribution to the October Revolution in Russia (see the Background timeline, 1917–1921), can you think of any reasons why Trotsky would not have been welcomed in many countries?

6   Using Sources 6 and 7 and the list of some of Trotsky's books written whilst he was in exile, write an attack on his activities and views from the viewpoint of a Soviet newspaper which is obviously supporting Stalin. You should include in your report:
    (a) Why Trotsky was expelled from Russia.
    (b) Why other countries will not have him for long.
    (c) His written attacks on your popular leader, Joseph Stalin.
    (d) His activities against the Soviet Union.
    (e) What should be done to punish Trotsky.

7   Trotsky himself was certain as to the 'author' of the attempt on his life of 23 May 1940 (Source 10). Imagine you were present when Colonel Salazar, head of Mexico's Secret Police, continued his interview with Trotsky by asking him what grounds (or evidence) he had to support his suspicions. Report Trotsky's answer as though you were Salazar's assistant.

The assassination

There is a great deal of mystery about the man who killed Leon Trotsky. His life and background are still unclear although historians have been able to discover some details of his activities before the assassination. In his twenty years' imprisonment following the murder, the killer never once revealed his true identity. He did, on the day of the assassination, carry with him a written 'confession' explaining why he thought Trotsky deserved to die. You will read extracts from this 'confession' later, but it will help you to know a little about the assassin and the way in which he was able to gain access to Trotsky.

It is known that 'Jacques Mornard' met one of Trotsky's American followers, called Sylvia Ageloff, in Paris, in 1938. She fell for him and they began a love affair which continued when both left France in early 1939. For a while 'Mornard' lived in Mexico whilst Sylvia stayed in New York. She joined him in January 1940 and introduced him to friends of Trotsky. By now the Trotskys lived in a small suburb called Coyoacan just outside Mexico City. Sylvia became one of Trotsky's secretaries. Gradually 'Mornard' managed to gain an invitation inside Trotsky's house by doing small favours for Trotsky's friends and becoming familiar with his guards. Having made himself known to the whole household, 'Mornard' took his opportunity to attack Trotsky on 20 August 1940. Trotsky died the next day. (See Sources 12 and 13.)

Source 11
Frank Jackson alias Jacques Mornard alias Ramon Mercader

photograph from The Prophet Outcast: Leon Trotsky, 1929–40, *Isaac Deutscher, Oxford, 1963)*

Source 12

ice-axe axe used by mountaineers to get a grip in icy conditions
infinitely neverending

I put my raincoat on the table on purpose, so that I could take out the *ice axe* which I had in the pocket . . . . at the exact moment when Trotsky started to read my article . . . I took the ice axe . . . . clenched it in my fist, and, closing my eyes, I gave him a tremendous blow on the head . . . . The man screamed in such a way as I will never forget it as long as I live. His scream was 'Aaaaa', very long, *infinitely* long, and it still seems to me as if that scream was piercing my brain. I saw Trotsky get up like a madman. He threw himself on me and bit my hand, then I pushed him so that he fell on the floor. He lifted himself up as best he could, and then, running or stumbling, I don't know how, he got out of the room.
from the Confession of 'Jacques Mornard' to the Mexican Police

Source 13

Mornard himself was in very poor physical condition. It was only on Trotsky's orders that he had not been killed. During the beating-up (by Trotsky's guards) he had said little; he just moaned 'Kill me, kill me', and 'They made me do it' and 'They have imprisoned my mother' . . . .
from 'The Assassination of Trotsky' (Christopher Weaver, 'History Today')

Source 14

The house where the murder took place – Leon Trotsky's villa at Coyoacan, near Mexico City.

Trotsky knew the assassin, Frank Jackson, personally for more than six months. Jackson enjoyed Trotsky's confidence because of his connection with Trotsky's movement in France and the United States. Jackson visited the house frequently. At no time did we have the least ground to suspect he was an agent of the GPU (Russian secret police.)

He entered the house on Aug. 20 at 5.30 o'clock. He met Mr Trotsky in the patio near the chicken yard, where he told Trotsky he had written an article on which he wished his advice. Trotsky agreed as a matter of course and walked with him to the dining room, where they met Mrs Trotsky. Jackson asked Mrs Trotsky for a glass of water, explaining his throat was dry. She offered him tea, since she and Trotsky had just finished their afternoon tea. He refused, taking only water.

Trotsky then invited Jackson into the study but without previously notifying his secretaries. The first indication of something wrong was the sound of terrible cries and a violent struggle in Trotsky's study. Secretary-guards at first thought an accident had occurred. The two who were closest immediately left their posts and rushed to the dining room next to Trotsky's study. Here they met Trotsky coming from the study with blood streaming down his face. One of the guards immediately attacked the assassin, who stood with a gun in his hand, and the other helped Trotsky . . . .

alpenstock ice-axe
assailant attacker

The assassin apparently struck Trotsky from behind with a miner's pick or *alpenstock* – the point penetrating into the brain. Instead of dropping unconscious as the assassin had evidently planned, Trotsky still retained consciousness and struggled with the *assailant*. As he lay bleeding on the floor later . . . . he told Hansen: 'Jackson shot me with a revolver, I am seriously wounded. I feel that this time it is the end.'

Hansen tried to convince him it was only a surface wound and could not have been caused by a revolver, because nobody heard a shot, but Trotsky replied: 'No, I feel here (pointing to his heart) that this time they have succeeded.'

from a written account by Joseph Hansen, one of Trotsky's American secretaries, in the New York Times, *22 August 1940*

Source 15
The instrument of murder – the weapon used to assassinate Trotsky. (Below)

(a) *Jackson/Mornard explained the manner in which he carried out the crime:* I had the idea of killing him seven or eight days beforehand. I had no definite plan. I wanted to kill him and then commit suicide afterwards . . . I found Trotsky feeding his rabbits . . . . He asked me if I had brought him an article I had

promised to write . . . . and invited me to his study . . . . While he was engaged in reading my article, I took the ice axe out of my raincoat and, closing my eyes, brought it down on his head . . . .

(b)   *Jackson/Mornard gives his reason for his crime:*

I understood that Trotsky was directly tied up with acts of terrorism and *sabotage* carried out in the USSR, I understood that he was betraying the only country where the revolution had triumphed. And that ended by *alienating* any feeling of sympathy I had for him.

(c)   *Opinion of the police investigators:*

This so-called Mornard was a member of the *Communist Militia of Catalonia* . . . No one knew where his money came from. He never seemed to do any work . . . . He was a petty adventurer without a future. Following the example of his mother, he became one of the *double instruments* of the GPU. Once in their hands, they decided that he should be the one to kill Trotsky . . . .

from an account by Colonel Salazar, the Chief of the Mexican Secret Police

Source 16

('Mornard' carried with him a letter explaining his motives for the assassination. Phrases in inverted commas are direct quotations from this letter.)

When he found himself face to face with Trotsky . . . . he had expected a great political leader 'directing the struggle of the liberation of the working class': instead he found a 'man who wished only to satisfy his desire for *vengeance* and hatred, and who used the workers' struggle simply as a means of hiding his own *paltriness* and selfish motives'.

Moreover, after he had been with Trotsky on several occasions, the letter continued, Mornard was told at last what was required of him. Trotsky proposed that he should go to Russia and there arrange a series of assassinations – first, that of Stalin. This, Mornard felt, was 'contrary to all the principles of a struggle which, until then, had been frank and open': and it 'destroyed his faith'.

sabotage deliberate damage done by spies or enemies

alienating removing

Communist Militia of Catalonia communist soldier from a part of Spain involved in the Civil War there

double-instruments double agents

vengeance revenge

paltriness worthlessness

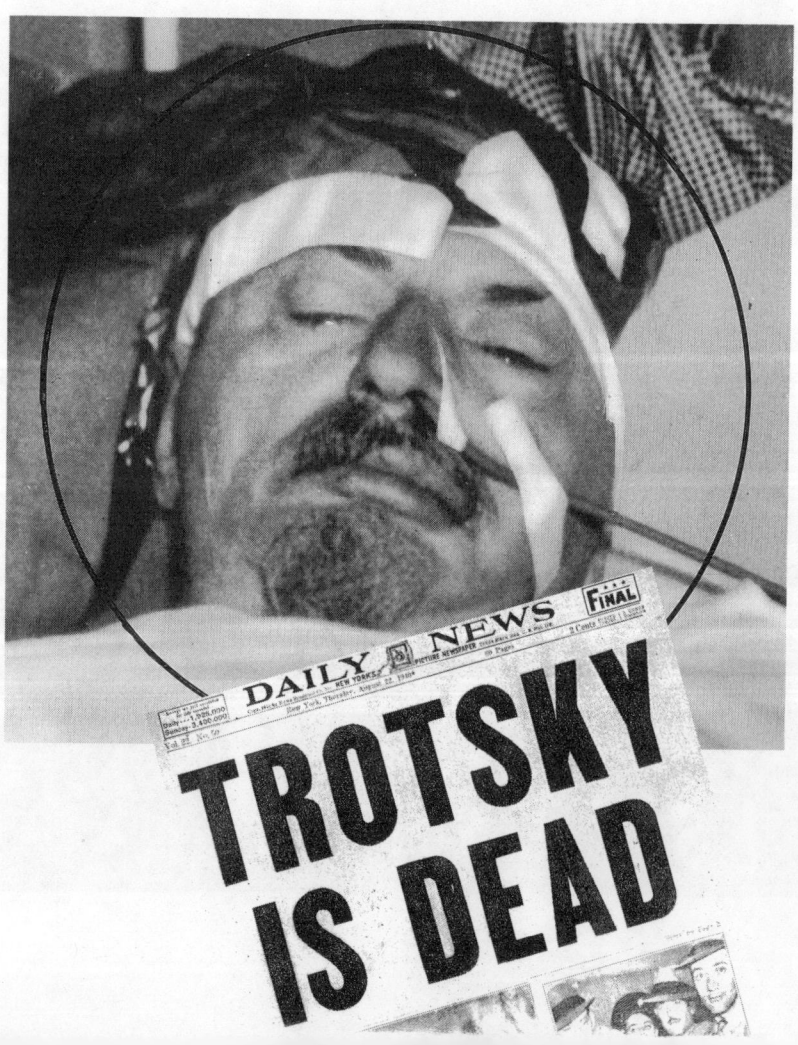

US newspaper report of Trotsky's death.

Finally, the letter said, Mornard had been driven to think of assassinating Trotsky because 'when I told him that I could not go to Russia because I wanted first to get married and that I could go only with my wife, he became upset and told me that I must have nothing more to do with her . . . and it was on this account, and for the sake of the 'young woman whom I love with all my heart' that he, Mornard, decided to 'sacrifice myself by getting rid of this leader of a workers' movement who has done nothing but harm it.'

from The Assassination of Trotsky (*Nicholas Mosley, Abacus, 1972*)

Source 17

('Mornard' *was questioned in great detail. He spent over 900 hours with psychiatrists alone.*)
(a)   It is ridiculous for a man to spend his days thinking about what he is going to do! I like to act and to solve my difficulties while I am acting! (His own words.)
(b)   *The psychiatrists*: 'He wanted to sacrifice himself for a great cause and yet at the same time built up an inner world which would protect him. He was weak and at the same time determined; and he showed no *remorse*.'

remorse guilt, sorrow

from a 1359–page report on 'Mornard' prepared by two Mexican psychiatrists

Source 18

His mother, Caridad, had gone to Moscow when she had heard that the assassination had been successful and she had received there from Stalin the Order of Lenin. She was also given the Order of the Hero of the Soviet Union to keep for her son.

from The Assassination of Trotsky (*Nicholas Mosley, Abacus, 1972*)

Source 19

Of Christ's twelve apostles Judas alone proved to be traitor. But if he had taken power, he would have shown the other eleven Apostles as traitors, and also the lesser Apostles whom Luke numbers as seventy.

from Stalin *by Leon Trotsky, published after his death (New York, 1946)*

Questions

8   Consider these theories surrounding the assassination of Trotsky:
(a) Stalin ordered the GPU (his secret service) to murder Trotsky.
(b) The murderer was mentally unbalanced and not wholly responsible for his actions.
(c) The killer had been encouraged by Trotsky to undertake operations against the Soviet Union such as the assassination of Stalin himself. In anger he turned on Trotsky.
Using the evidence provided, explain in your own words the arguments in favour of each of the these theories.

9   Which do you think is the most well-supported explanation? Give at least three reasons.

10

Trotsky was a threat to Stalin's position both inside and outside the USSR.	Trotsky was organising a *Communist International* in direct competition to Stalin.	Trotsky had played a far more vital role in the October 1917 Revolution than Stalin.
Stalin had eliminated most of his enemies. Trotsky was the last really important 'rival' still alive.	Communism had lost in Spain in 1939 and was under attack from Fascists and Nazis in Europe.	Europe was already involved in the Second World War and Stalin was afraid of an attack upon the USSR by Nazi Germany.

The grid shows some of the threats facing Stalin in 1940 when Trotsky was assassinated. Use the grid and any other evidence to which you wish to refer, to write a summary of Mornard's role against the background of world events. Why were his actions so important at that time?

5 Nazi propaganda - 'The war that Hitler won'?

Introduction

One of the most important skills of history and one which is also of great value in life outside school is to be able to recognise the differences between various *types* of statements. You may be asked to consider a statement of *fact*. On the other hand people may also give their *opinions* on a particular happening or topic. The problem is that some people confuse facts with opinions and vice-versa. They may feel they are stating a fact when what they are giving is an opinion.

A fact is something which is known to be true and can be supported by the available evidence. An opinion, on the other hand, is a belief which might be held by one or more persons. Usually, if you have an opinion, you would select or choose facts to support your view. It is a strange thing that two people who hold different views may well be able to use the same facts to support their opinions! (Perhaps you can give examples?) It is, then, a question of how you interpret the facts. Sometimes attempts will be made to persuade you that a particular opinion is the right one. We call this propaganda.

Background

During the period 1933 to 1945 the Nazi (National Socialist) Party ruled over Germany. The Nazis were keen to win over the German people to their views, opinions and policies. Hitler appointed Doctor Josef Goebbels as Minister for *Popular Enlightenment* and Propaganda soon after coming to power.

Dr Joseph Goebbels, 'Minister for Popular Enlightenment and Propaganda', with his leader, Hitler. What impression does the photograph convey of the two men?

popular aimed at the
    majority of ordinary
    people
enlightenment making these
    people aware of the
    'truth' of Nazi beliefs

Goebbels wanted to make use of every known method to spread the Nazi message. In this exercise you will investigate some of these methods, but first you should consider why Hitler and his followers thought propaganda was so important. Once you know what Hitler's aims were for Nazi propaganda, you might be able to judge the success of the methods used.

The aims of Nazi propaganda

Source 1

the masses the ordinary
    people
slogans catchwords or
    phrases easily
    remembered

The understanding of *the masses* is very small and their intelligence is feeble. On the other hand, they quickly forget . . . . All effective propaganda must be kept to a very few facts and must express these as far as possible in *slogans*. These slogans must be repeated constantly until the very last member of the public understands what you want him to understand by your slogan . . . . the first rule of all propaganda is . . . the one-sided attitude it must take towards every question it deals with . . . . What, for example, would we say about a poster that was supposed to advertise a new soap and that described other soaps as good? We would only shake our heads. The same applies to political advertising.
from Mein Kampf *(My Struggle) A. Hitler (English translation London 1939)*

Source 2

The aim of propaganda is not to show differing sides on views that do not agree, each given the same amount of coverage, but rather to emphasise only the position *we* are taking. Propaganda must not investigate the truth from all sides. It was a great mistake to discuss the question of who was responsible for the (First World) war and say that Germany alone could not be blamed. The sole responsibility should have been laid on the shoulders of the enemy without any discussion whatsoever.
from Mein Kampf *(My Struggle) A. Hitler (English translation, London 1939)*

Source 3

(a) I see in the newly formed Ministry for Popular Enlightenment and Propaganda a link between Government and people . . . . It must see its . . . task as making all the necessary propaganda preparations to win the whole people over to its side.
(b) . . . . propaganda is not an end (achievement) in itself but a means to an end. We are setting up here a Propaganda ministry that does not exist for its own sake . . . . but one which is a means to an end . . . . The purpose of our Movement was to prepare people, to organise people and to win them over to the idea of the National (Socialist) Revolution. That end . . . has been achieved and so the verdict has been passed on our propaganda methods.
Dr Josef Goebbels in a speech to the representatives of the press, 1933

Source 4

This new Reich will give its youth to no one, but will itself take youth and give it its own education and its own upbringing.
Adolf Hitler in a speech on 1 May 1937

Source 5

The Third Reich the Third
    German Empire, Hitler's
    Empire

The leadership of Germany increasingly believes that schools have to be open for the spread of our beliefs. To carry out this task we know of no better means than the film. The film is particularly important for school children. Film education must not only make clear modern political problems but it must also provide children with a knowledge of Germany's heroic past and a deep understanding of the future development of the *Third Reich.*
Dr Bernard Rust, Minister of Education, in a speech to an invited audience of teachers, 1934

Questions

1   Examine Sources 1 and 2. According to Hitler,
    (a) What is the general purpose of propaganda?
    (b) What makes propaganda successful?
2   What did Goebbels think was his main task as Minister for Popular Enlightenment and Propaganda? (Source 3).
3   (a) Why was it so important that the Nazis won the minds of the young?

(b) What three aspects of German life did Dr Rust think children ought to be aware
     of?

Film propaganda

Source 6

Our State has given the film a very important assignment; it is therefore one of the
most valuable factors in the National Education . . . .
Josef Goebbels to a Hitler Youth audience, 1941

The Nazis were so keen to use films as propaganda that they set up a 'Film Hour
for the Young' or 'Jugendfilmstunde' which was organised by the *Hitler Youth*.

Source 7

Film attendance and performances of the Youth Film Hours, 1934–43

Year	Performances	Attendance
1934–5	–	300 000
1935–6	905	425 176
1936–7	1 725	879 839
1937–8	3 563	1 771 236
1938–9	4 886	2 561 489
1939–40	8 244	3 538 224
1940–1	12 560	4 800 000
1941–2	15 800	5 600 000
1942–3	over 45 290	11 215 000

from Youth and Film *(A. J. Sander, Berlin, 1944)*

Source 8

censor one who controls
   what appears on film,
   TV, radio or in
   publications
omitted left out
glorify praise
racially inferior a lower race
   or type of people

The party realised that new technology could get the message across to every
German by controlling the newspapers, the radio and the cinema. Goebbels acted
as a *censor*. He licensed every film before any work on it could begin. Often he
would read a script and make notes suggesting which scenes should be
omitted . . . .

The party tried to get certain ideas across in films. It was to be shown to be
glorious to die for Germany, not just in war, but if necessary by suicide if one was
suffering an incurable disease. In early films the dangers of communism were
shown. Later films were used to *glorify* the German nation; show the Jews as
racially inferior; . . . . and of course . . . . to praise Hitler and encourage fitness
and greater industrial production. In the film *Kolberg* the German commander,
Gneisenau, comes to the town of Kolberg which is surrounded by French troops.
He meets Nettelbeck, the town's mayor, and has the following conversation:

*(The film is set in the early 1800s, during Napoleon's invasions of German
territory.)*

GNEISENAU: 35 000 men, Nettelbeck, and at least 500 guns and all directed against
     this town. Do you realise what that means? Compared with this everything
     we've experienced up to now is child's play.

NETTELBECK: Commander, will you please tell me frankly what you are trying to
     say.

GNEISENAU: We are finished, Nettelbeck, it's senseless to go on. We cannot hold the
     town.

NETTELBECK: And?

GNEISENAU: Surrender, Nettelbeck!

Magdeburg, Erfurt, Stettin,
   Spandau German towns
   captured at this time by
   Napoleon

NETTELBECK: Oh yes, like *Magdeburg, Erfurt, Stettin and Spandau*. It was all in
     vain then? The end – dishonour?

GNEISENAU: There is no dishonour when soldiers have fired their last bullet. Even
     Blücher* had to *capitulate*.

NETTELBECK: But, commander, we haven't fired our last bullet. And after all
     Blücher did not have to surrender the town he was born in. You were not born
     in Kolberg, Gneisenau. You were ordered to Kolberg. But we grew up here. We

know every stone, every street corner, every house. So we won't let go now! And even if we have to hang on to the soil of our town with our fingernails, we won't let go. No, they will have to hack our hands off one by one, kill us one after the other. Gneisenau, you can't expect an old man like me to dishonour himself by handing our town over to Napoleon. And I have promised our King too. Better be buried under the ruins than *capitulate*. Gneisenau, Gneisenau, I have never gone on my knees to anyone before. Now I'm doing it. Gneisenau, Kolberg must not be surrendered!

capitulate surrender

GNEISENAU: That is what I wanted to hear from you, Nettelbeck. Now we can die together.

(*Blücher was a Prussian (German) General who helped to finally defeat Napoleon at the battle of Waterloo.)

from The Nazi Cinema *(Irwin Leiser, Secker and Warburg, 1974)*

Source 9

A film poster advertising the film, Hitler Youth Quex.

Plot of the feature film Hitler Youth Quex

In a tough, Communist-dominated working-class district of Berlin, the theft of an apple sets off a riot which is firmly suppressed by the police. One of the injured, an unemployed worker called Volker, is helped home by his Communist friend Stoppel. Recovering and feeling like a drink, Volker starts to beat up his wife when she refuses to give him money. Frau Volker is saved by the arrival of their young son Heini, a printer's apprentice, who offers the money he has earned for overtime.

At Stoppel's invitation, Heini joins a camping expedition of the Communist Youth, but is disgusted by the roughness and rowdiness of the Communist kids – and much impressed by a nearby camp of smart, disciplined Hitler Youth (HJ or Hitlerjugend). Back home in Berlin he gets to know some members of the Hitler Youth, and warns them of a plan that he's overheard among the Communists to wreck their new local HJ headquarters. When the 'Reds' learn that Heini has spilt the beans, they swear to get him – and his distraught mother, hearing of this, tries to gas herself and the boy. He is saved by neighbours, but she dies.

When Heini is recovering in hospital, his HJ friends come and present him with the HJ uniform he has longed for; and their Group Leader Kass, convinces him in an argument with his father that national loyalty is the only kind that matters. As soon as he is well enough, Heini goes to work at the HJ club, preparing leaflets for a forthcoming Nazi meeting. He volunteers to distribute these in the heart of the 'Red' district – which is where his Communist enemies eventually corner and kill him.

Questions

4   Look at the figures in Source 7.
     (a) What effect did the Second World War (1939–45) have on the number of performances of Nazi films for youth?
     (b) Can you think of any reasons why this should be so? Explain your reasons.
5   How did Goebbels try to control what was written, said or shown for the public in Nazi Germany?
6   (a) Irwin Leiser (Source 8) tells us that the Nazis wanted to get *seven* main ideas across in films. What were these?
     (b) Which of the above ideas do you think (i) *Kolberg* (Source 8) and (ii) *Hitler Youth Quex* (Source 9) tried to get across? In each case explain how the films tried to do this.

Nazi propaganda posters

Someone living in Nazi Germany during the early 1930s would have noticed a steady increase in the number of posters appearing in public places, magazines and newspapers, advertising the aims and beliefs of the party. This became a flood after 1934 when the Nazis took complete control over the country. The 'message' of individual posters was usually obvious and direct. Symbols were used to make a point. Nazis were strong, firm-jawed, athletic and clean-cut. Enemies were shown as inferior, weak, crafty and immoral.

Of course, once Nazi Germans began taking control of other countries in the early 1940s, Austria first and then Czechoslovakia, Poland, Holland, Belgium, France and many others, they introduced to each of them their propaganda posters. These were designed to show that the Germans were their 'real' friends and the enemies of Germany were also the foes of the conquered countries.

In the pages that follow you will find a selection of Nazi posters. Take one poster at a time and investigate it thoroughly using the following list of questions to help you.

    (i)   Who is the poster aimed at? (i.e. which nationality or which 'section' or class of people)

    (ii) What symbols or effects are used to put the message across?

    (iii) What is the message or point of the poster?

    (iv) Is it effective? Does it seem to you to work?

Remember that symbols or effects *represent* an idea or try to give an impression of the an idea. Look out for these examples:

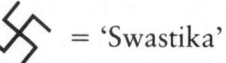 = 'Swastika' – symbol of the Nazi Party

 = 'Hammer and sickle' – symbol of Communist Russia

British bulldog – symbol of Great Britain (and sometimes Winston Churchill!)
Motherland/Fatherland – what many Germans thought of their country.

Source 10
Nazi election poster of 1932

National Socialism – the organised will of the Nation.

Source 11
A German poster of 1934

Deutschland is Germany and the banner contains the slogan, Loyalty, Honour and Order.

Source 12
A German poster of 1941: 'Welcome men on the dole. Millions of kids without a future. Save the German family. Vote for Adolf Hitler.'

„Und gegen diesen grau-
samen, bestialischen, tie-
rischen Gegner, gegen
diesen Gegner mit seiner
gewaltigen Rüstung,
haben unsere Soldaten
ihre gewaltigen Siege
erkämpft.

Ich weiß kein Wort, das
ihrer Leistung gerecht
werden könnte. Was sie
an Mut und Tapferkeit
hier dauernd vollbrin-
gen, an unermeßlichen
Anstrengungen das ist
unvorstellbar!"

Source 13
*A propaganda poster
of 1943. The text reads
in part: (top left)
'... this awful,
bestial, subhuman
enemy...'; (top
right) '...
courage and bravery
and immeasurable
striving...'.*

Source 14 (left)
*A propaganda poster
of 1944. The text
lists defeats and
humiliations suffered
by the French at
English hands from
1300 to 1942 and
asks, 'What awaits us
next?'*

Rallies, marches and demonstrations

Source 15

pennants flags

'The Führer is coming!' A ripple went through the crowds. Around the speakers' platform one could see hands raised in the Hitler salute . . . . A second speaker welcomed Hitler and made way for the man who had drawn 120 000 people of all classes and ages. There stood Hitler in a simple black coat and looked over the crowd, waiting – a forest of swastika *pennants* swished up . . . . His voice was hoarse after all his speaking during the previous days. When the speech was over there was roaring enthusiasm and applause.

Frau (Mrs) Luise Solmitz, a Hamburg schoolteacher, describing her impressions of a Nazi rally on 23 April 1932

Source 16

exerted an influence spread a feeling
tremor shaking, quiver

Hundreds of swastika banners filed in to the impressive music of the 'Song of the Standards' and formed a solid mass of red and gold at the back of the stage. Every device of music and coloured light was used to keep the atmosphere tense and the spotlight that played on the giant swastika behind the banners *exerted an influence* that was almost hypnotic.

   The atmosphere was most strained and unreal. The speakers deliberately played on the feelings of the people . . . . when something particularly impressive was read out, a curious *tremor* swept the crowd and all around me individuals uttered a strange cry, a kind of emotional sigh that invariably changed into a shout of 'Heil Hitler'.

Stephen H. Roberts of the University of Sydney, Australia, recalling the atmosphere at one rally in 1936

Source 17

hysterics people who have lost control over their actions
moat ditch
Messiah one chosen to lead his people to greatness – a Christ-like figure
transformed completely changed
swooned fainted

Nuremberg, 4 Sept 1934.
About ten o'clock tonight I got caught in a mob of ten thousand *hysterics* who jammed the *moat* in front of Hitler's hotel shouting: 'We want our Führer'. I was a little shocked at the faces, especially those of the women, when Hitler finally appeared on the balcony for a moment . . . . They looked at him as if he were a *Messiah*, their faces *transformed* into something . . . . inhuman. If he had remained in sight for more than a few moments, I think many of the women would have *swooned* from excitement.

from Berlin Diary *by William Shirer, an American newspaper reporter*

Source 18
Nazi rally in Nuremberg in 1934

Source 19
'Day of the Labour Service' in Nuremberg, 1937

Source 20
A torchlit parade in Berlin to celebrate the end of the fifth anniversary of the Nazi takeover in Germany

Questions

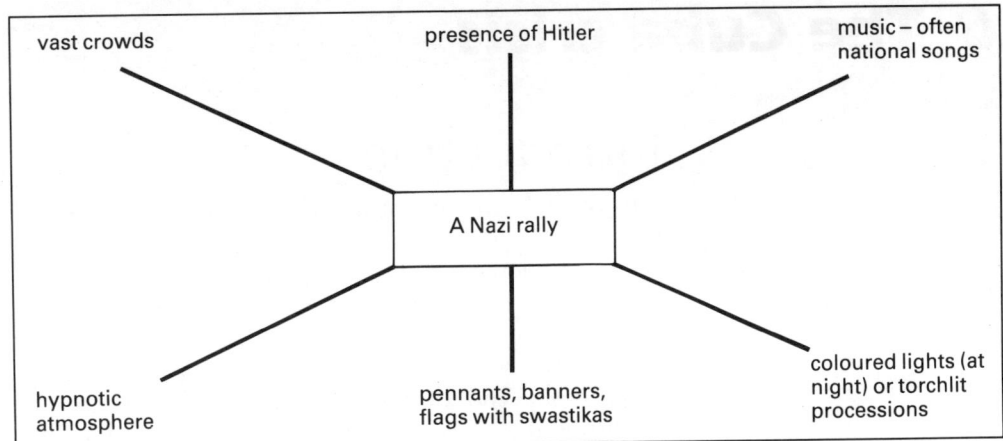

7   Use the diagram to explain why rallies, parades and demonstrations were so *different* from other types of propaganda.

8   Which do you think were most useful to the Nazis in their propaganda efforts:
films?
posters?
rallies?
Give reasons for your choice.

9   German propaganda methods seem to have worked. Hitler and the other Nazi leaders gained complete control in Germany and led the German people into the Second World War.
   Using any of the sources provided, suggest ways the Nazis might have planned and carried out a propaganda compaign in *two* of the following situations:
(i)   in trying to gain political control over a particular area or city in Germany.
(ii) in trying to persuade a conquered people that life under the Nazis was better for them.
(iii) in trying to increase the confidence and efficiency of the armed forces.
(iv) in trying to persuade the Germans, as the war drew to a close, that they should be prepared to die for their country.
(v)   in trying to show that their enemies were aggressive, cruel and evil.

In both of the situations you choose, explain *why* you feel that the methods suggested would be effective.

NB Remember that TV was not available at the time but radios were fairly common.

6 The Cuba crisis

Introduction

devastate destroy

One of the skills of history which is also useful to life outside school is to be able to see both sides of an argument. It is very tempting sometimes to see only one point of view and not to recognise that someone else might think or feel differently. This attitude is not confined to individual people – whole nations sometimes act as though theirs is the only truth and any country which does not agree with their version is obviously wrong.

Since the end of the Second World War in 1945, the two most powerful countries in the world have been the United States of America (USA) and the Union of Soviet Socialist Republics (USSR). More than any other powers, these two play a vital part (or 'role') in keeping the world at peace. Between them they have sufficient nuclear weapons to completely *devastate* our planet, causing billions of deaths and making large parts of the earth uninhabitable.

Just imagine a situation in which these 'superpowers' refused to see each other's point of view – in which each believed that it was right and was prepared to risk a nuclear war to prove it! This seemed to the rest of the world to be a real possibility in the autumn of 1962.

The most powerful men in the world, President John F. Kennedy of the USA and Premier Nikita Khrushchev of the Soviet Union seen during their summit talks in Vienna in 1961.

Background

Cuba is a small island situated in the Caribbean Sea in a very important position between the southernmost extent of the USA, the northern coast of South America and, to its west, the small states of Central America. At its nearest point to the USA, it is less than 150 miles from Florida. It had for centuries been controlled by Spain and only in 1898 did the island achieve its independence from that country after a bloody revolution.

Having thrown out the Spanish, Cuba began to depend more and more for its trade and economy on the USA. Many companies from the USA set up branches in Cuba, attracted by cheap labour and the island's few, but important natural resources. Most of the best sugar-growing land was in the hands of US businessmen, who also controlled half the railways and most of the electricity and telephone services.

In order to protect all the money it was investing in the island's economy, the USA supported *dictators* who, it believed, would at least keep the country stable, peaceful and settled. From 1933 to 1958, the brutal dictatorship of a man called Batista was responsible for an era of corruption and terror and growing hostility towards the USA which supported him.

In 1958 Batista was overthrown by resistance fighters under a man called Fidel Castro. Relations between Cuba and the USA became very bad as Castro took

dictators rulers who have absolute authority and can run a country without a parliament, elections, etc.

Dr Fidel Castro, the Cuban Leader.

lands and factories from US companies and brought them under Cuban control. The USA responded by banning sugar imports from the island. Castro was gradually coming to adopt a communist position and began to turn to the Soviet Union for Cuba's economic needs.

In April 1961, Cuban opponents of Castro who had fled the country tried to invade the island. They were supported with arms and money from the USA. Setting out from a base in Guatemala they landed at the Bay of Pigs in the south of Cuba. The force was easily defeated by Castro's army but the Cuban leader now regarded the threat to his country from the USA as very serious indeed.

In order to protect Cuba's independence he asked the USSR to supply him with defensive weapons. However, US *reconnaissance* aircraft took photographs which indicated to the US President, John F. Kennedy, that some of these weapons were not *defensive*, but *offensive*. He claimed that the Russian leader, Khrushchev, was supplying Castro with long-range missiles which could threaten the USA.

The build-up to the crisis

On Tuesday morning, October 16, 1962, shortly after nine o'clock, President Kennedy called and asked to come to the White House. He said only that we were facing great trouble. Shortly afterward, in his office, he told me that a U-2 had just finished a photographic mission and that the *Intelligence Community* had become convinced tht Russia was placing missiles and atomic weapons in Cuba.

That was the begining of the Cuban missile crisis – a *confrontation* between the two giant atomic nations, the United States and the USSR, which brought the world to the *abyss* of nuclear destruction and the end of mankind. From that moment in President Kennedy's office until Sunday morning, October 28, that was my life – and for Americans and Russians, for the whole world, it was *their* life, as well.

from 13 Days (*Robert F. Kennedy, Watts, 1968*). *Robert F. Kennedy was John F. Kennedy's brother. The book was published after the assassination of both John and Robert Kennedy.*

---

reconnaissance 'spy' aircraft which survey an area from the air
defensive for the defence of a country
offensive to attack other countries

Source 1
Intelligence Community People who look after the security of the USA and gather the information thought necessary for this
confrontation quarrel
abyss bottomless pit

Source 2
Photographic evidence collected by U-2 reconnaissance planes from a height of 14 miles over Cuba

MISSILE ERECTOR

5 TRUCKS UNDER CAMOUFLAGE NETTING

CABLE

THEODOLITE STATION

5 TRUCKS UNDER CAMOUFLAGE NETTIN

MISSILE SHELTER TENTS

Source 3
*Map showing the range
of the Soviet missiles in
Cuba*

Key
IRBM Intercontinental
range ballistic
missile
MRBM Medium range
ballistic missile

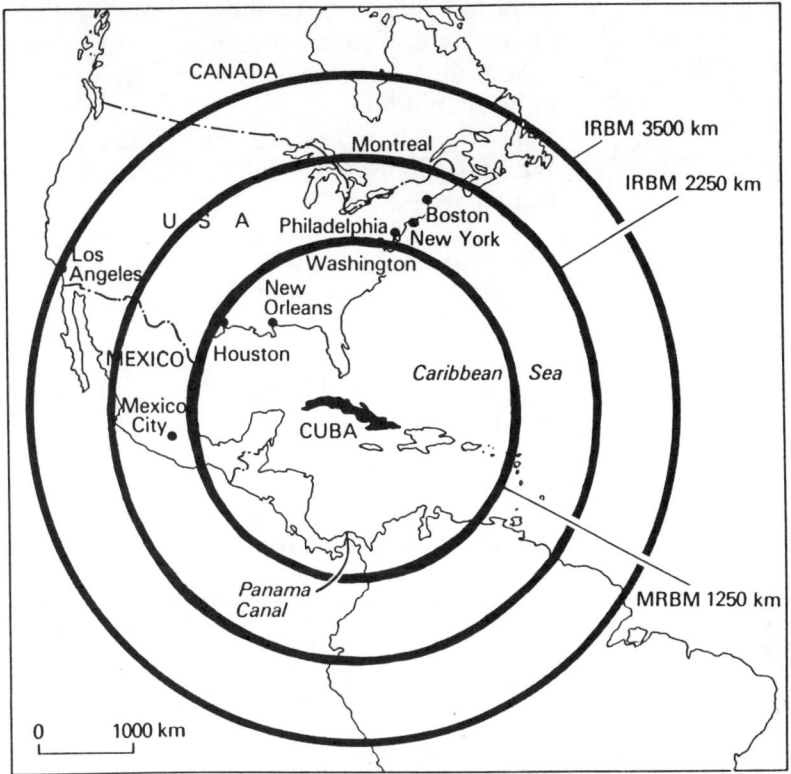

The view of the USA

Source 4

quarantine/blockade
stopping any contact
with a particular country
by land, sea or air
advocate one in favour of
installations structures, sites
current ICBM capacity the
total number of
long-range missiles
possessed by the USSR
deployed spread out
Strategic Air Command the
United States Air Force

(i) The general feeling in the beginning was that some form of action was required. There were those, although they were a small minority, who felt the missiles did not alter the balance of power and therefore necessitated no action. Most felt, at that stage, that an air strike against the missile sites could be the only course . . . . It was during the afternoon and evening of that first day, Tuesday (Oct. 16), that we began to discuss the idea of a *quarantine* or *blockade*. Secretary McNamara, by Wednesday, became the blockade's strongest *advocate*.

(ii) An examination of photography taken on Wednesday, 17 October, showed several other *installations*, with at least sixteen and possibly thirty-two missiles of over 1000 mile range. Our military experts advised that these missiles could be in operation within a week. The next day, Thursday, estimates by our Intelligence Community placed in Cuba missiles with an atomic-warhead potential of about one-half the *current ICBM* capacity of the entire Soviet Union. The photography having indicated that the missiles were being directed at certain American cities, the estimate was that within a few minutes of their being fired 80 million Americans would be dead.

(iii) Missile crews were placed on maximum alert. Troops were moved into Florida and the southeastern part of the United States . . . . The Navy *deployed* 180 ships into the Caribbean. The *Strategic Air Command* was dispersed to civilian landing fields around the country . . . . The B-52 bomber force was ordered into the air fully loaded with atomic weapons. As one came down to land, another immediately took its place in the air.

from 13 Days *(Robert F. Kennedy, Watts, 1968)*

Source 5

This nation is opposed to war. We are also true to our word. Our unswerving objective, therefore, must be to prevent the use of these missiles against this or any other country . . . . I have directed that the following initial steps be taken immediately:

First: . . . . a strict quarantine on all offensive military equipment under ship-

surveillance watching,
spying upon
Western Hemisphere in this
case, 'the West', the USA
and its allies

provocative likely to lead
to violent action

ment to Cuba . . . . All ships of any kind bound for Cuba from whatever nation or port will, if found to contain cargoes of offensive weapons, be turned back.

Second: . . . . continued and increased close *surveillance* of Cuba and its military buildup . . . .

Third: . . . . any nuclear missile launched from Cuba against any nation in the *Western Hemisphere* (will be regarded) as an attack by the Soviet Union on the United States.

(Fourth, fifth and sixth not relevant to the investigation)

Seventh and finally: I call upon Chairman Khrushchev to halt . . . this . . . reckless and *provocative* threat to world peace . . . .

from President Kennedy's radio/TV report to the American people, 22 October 1962

Questions

1   Use Sources 1–3 to write a paragraph explaining the threat to world peace that the USA claimed was coming from Cuba.
2   What evidence did the USA use to support its claims?
3   (a) According to Robert Kennedy, the President's brother (Source 4), what three courses of action were open to the USA?
       (b) Which option did President Kennedy choose (Source 5)? Why do you think he made this decision?
4   What phrase in Source 5 shows who President Kennedy thought was responsible for the crisis?

The Russian view

Source 6

destinies fate

. . . . who gave the United States the right to assume the role of ruler of the *destinies* of other countries and peoples? Why must the Cubans conduct the internal affairs of their country not as they see fit but as the United States prefers? Cuba belongs to the Cuban people and only it can be master of its fate . . . . In this anxious hour the Soviet government considers itself duty-bound to seriously warn the government of the United States that in carrying out the measures announced by President Kennedy, it is recklessly playing with fire and taking a grave responsibility for the fate of the world . . . .

Who believes that Cuba can threaten the United States? If the size, resources and weapons of both countries are compared, no statesman in his right mind could see Cuba as a threat to the United States or to any other country . . . .

The United States has stopped at nothing, not even the organisation of the armed attack on Cuba of April 1961 (i.e. the Bay of Pigs incident, see Background), to deprive the Cuban people of the freedom and independence it had won . . . . and to make Cuba an American puppet.

from a Soviet Government statement of 23 October 1962

Source 7

. . . . if indeed war should break out, then it would not be in our power to stop it . . . I have taken part in two wars and know that war ends when it has rolled through cities and villages, everywhere sowing death and destruction . . . . Only lunatics or suicides, who themselves want to die and to destroy the whole world before they die could do this . . . . if assurances were given that the President of the United States would not permit an attack on Cuba, and the blockade lifted, then the question of the removal or the destruction of the missile sites in Cuba would then be an entirely different question . . . . This is my proposal. No more weapons to Cuba and those within Cuba withdrawn or destroyed, and you respond by ending your blockade and also agree not to invade Cuba. Do not interfere in a *piratical* way with Russian ships . . . .

piratical like pirates

from a letter from Khrushchev received by President Kennedy on 26 October 1962

Source 8

Your rockets are situated in Britain, situated in Italy, and are aimed against us. Your rockets are situated in Turkey. You are worried by Cuba. You say that it worries you because it is a distance of 90 miles by sea from the coast of America, but Turkey is next to us. Our sentries walk up and down and look at each other.

Do you consider then that you have the right to demand security for your own country and the removal of those weapons which you call offensive and do not acknowledge the same right for us?

I therefore make this proposal: We agree to remove from Cuba those means which you regard as offensive means; we agree to carry this out and make a pledge in the United Nations. Your representatives will make a declaration to the effect that the United States, on its part, considering the uneasiness and anxiety of the Soviet state, will remove its similar means from Turkey.

from a further letter from the Soviet Government to President Kennedy, received on 27 October 1962

The end of the crisis

Source 9

rendered inoperable made incapable of working

I have read your letter of 26 October with great care, and welcomed the statement of your desire to seek a prompt solution to the problem. The first thing that needs to be done, however, is for work to cease on offensive missile bases in Cuba and for all weapons systems in Cuba capable of offensive use to be *rendered inoperable*, under effective UN arrangements. Assuming this is done promptly I have given my representatives in New York instructions that will permit them to work out this week-end . . . an arrangement for a permanent solution to the Cuban problem along the lines suggested in your letter of 26 October.

As I read your letter, the key elements of your proposals – which seem generally acceptable as I understand them – are as follows:
(1) You would agree to remove these weapons systems from Cuba under appropriate UN observation and supervision; and undertake, with suitable safeguards, to halt the further introduction of such weapons systems into Cuba.
(2) We, on our part, would agree – upon the establishment of adequate arrangements through the UN to ensure the carrying out and continuation of these commitments –
    (a) to remove promptly the quarantine measures now in effect; and
    (b) to give assurances against an invasion of Cuba. I am confident that other nations of the Western hemisphere would be prepared to do likewise.

President Kennedy, in a letter to Krushchev on 27 October 1962

Source 10

dismantle take apart
detente improvement in relations; coming together
prohibition refusal to allow
thermonuclear that explode using very high temperatures

(i) I regard with respect and trust the statement you made in your message of 27 October 1962 that there would be no attack, no invasion of Cuba . . . then the motives which forced us to give assistance of such a kind to Cuba disappear. It is for this reason that we instructed our officers . . . . to take appropriate actions to stop the construction of the (missile) facilities, to *dismantle* them and return them to the Soviet Union.
(ii) In conclusion, I should like to say something about a *detente* between Nato and the Warsaw Treaty countries that you have mentioned. We have spoken about this long since and are prepared to continue to exchange views on this question with you and to find a reasonable solution.

We should like to proceed with discussions on the *prohibition* of atomic and *thermonuclear* weapons, general disarmament, and other problems . . . .

from Khrushchev's letter to Kennedy of 28 October 1962

The results of the Cuba crisis

Source 11

John F. Kennedy had won. While he and the rest of America's leaders were asleep, the crisis passed . . . . The Soviet government was backing down. It had agreed to dismantle its missile installations and take them home . . . The Russians did dismantle the bases. They took everything away and bulldozed the installations into rubble . . . . It should be noted that three months after the crisis, the United States removed all its missiles from Turkey and Italy, and sixty of its Thor (missiles) from Britain . . . .   *(continued overleaf)*

Certain signs of a thaw appeared in the Cold war . . . .
from The Brink *(David Detzer, Dent, 1980)*

Soviet missiles and transporters being shipped back to the USSR from Cuba.

Source 12

We sent the Americans a note saying that we agreed to remove our missiles and bombers on the condition that the President give us his assurance that there would be no invasion of Cuba by the forces of the United States or anybody else. Finally Kennedy gave in and agreed to make a statement giving us such an assurance . . . . It has been, to say the least, an interesting and challenging situation. The two most powerful nations of the world had been squared off against each other, each with its finger on the button . . . . It was a great victory for us though . . . a triumph of Soviet foreign policy . . . a spectacular success without having to fire a single shot!
from Khrushchev Remembers *(Deutsch, 1974)*

A demonstration in London against US policy on Cuba. Scenes like this were seen in towns and cities around the world.

Questions

5   Using the background information together with Sources 6 and 7, explain why Cuba felt threatened by the USA.

6   What other arguments does Khrushchev put forward in Source 8 to defend the USSR's shipment of weapons to Cuba?

7   What suggestions does Khrushchev make in Sources 7 and 8 to end the crisis?

8   What is Kennedy's reaction to Khrushchev's proposals (Source 9)?

9   'For a few days the world seemed on the verge of a major nuclear war. But Khrushchev gave way: he agreed to the withdrawal of the missiles and the dismantling of the bases, and the Americans agreed not to invade Cuba.' (R. D. Cornwell, 1984)
How does this statement by a modern British writer contradict Khrushchev's view in Source 12?

10 Who do you think really won a victory? Justify your answer by giving reasons.

7 Reactions to oppression

Introduction

People react to a situation in different ways. When something happens, a piece of good news, for example, even members of a family or close friends may not react in the same manner. This is probably even more true when events or personalities are distant and do not affect us directly. Reports of famine, terrorism, natural disasters or space exploration draw different responses from groups and individuals with varying backgrounds and attitudes.

The object of this study is to help you to consider how an important human issue has provoked completely different reactions from groups and individuals directly involved in the situation. In this exercise you are going to investigate the problem of 'oppression'. For the purposes of this enquiry you should interpret 'oppression' as the putting-down of the people of a country, or at least of many people in the country, by authority based on force.

You should remember that we are not here considering the question of whether these people are, in fact, oppressed, but how they or their representatives and leaders have responded to the injustices *they feel* are being committed.

In each case study you will be presented with a brief background survey to help you see how the feeling of oppression grew. The following cases will be considered:

(i) Non-cooperation and civil disobedience in India, 1918–48.
(ii) The Palestine Liberation Organisation, 1956 to the present.
(iii) Solidarity – Poland's 'Free Trade Union', 1980 to the present.

Case Study 1
A non-violent response – India 1918–48

India was brought into the growing British Empire during the seventeenth and eighteenth centuries. In a series of wars against its main European rival, France, and against Indian princes, Britain finally gained control of 'the jewel in the crown'.

Possession of India brought many benefits. Britain was anxious to protect its profitable colony and made every effort to ensure that other great powers did not interfere. Throughout the nineteenth century the security of India was a key consideration in the planning of the British Government, even to the point of buying control of the newly-built Suez Canal in 1878 in order to safeguard the sea-route to India.

India itself had presented few problems to the British as its people were divided by race, class and religion. Britain was therefore unprepared for the problems which arose at the end of the First World War in 1918 when, for the first time, a 'national movement' (that is, a movement devoted to winning freedom from foreign rule), began to threaten her control. The leader of this movement was Mohandas Karamchand Gandhi and he and his followers wanted a united and independent India free from British rule. The British then were regarded by Indian *nationalists* as oppressors.

nationalists people who put the interests and independence of their country above everything

Gandhi's methods were new and remarkable. In order to understand his approach, you need to know that he was a very religious man who saw violence as being unsatisfactory and unnecessary in most situations. He followed the idea of *satyagraha*, which means 'truth-force'. His belief was that non-violence and willingly-accepted suffering in search of truth, would succeed where violent methods might not.

Source 1

(i) When a person claims to be non-violent, he is expected not to be angry with one who has injured him. He will not wish him harm; he will wish him well; he

Mahatma Gandhi in London in 1931. He is dressed in his usual simple way, despite the fact that he is meeting the British Prime Minister.

will not swear at him; he will not cause him any physical hurt. He will put up with all the injury to which he is subjected by the wrongdoer. Thus non-violence is complete innocence. Complete non-violence is complete absence of ill-will against all that lives . . . . We must not intend harm to the English or to our *cooperating countrymen*, if and whilst we claim to be non-violent.

cooperating countrymen those Indians who cooperated with the British

(ii) Therefore, whilst we are pursuing the policy of non-violence, we are bound to be actively friendly to English administrators and their cooperators. I felt ashamed when I was told that in some parts of India it was not safe for Englishmen or well-known cooperators to move about safely.

from an article written by Gandhi for the magazine Young India, *1922*

Source 2

(An example of a *satyagraha* . . . . or 'non-cooperation' with the British – in the district of Kaira in 1918.)

We the undersigned . . . . solemnly declare that we shall not pay the assessment* for the year whether it be wholly or in part; we shall leave it to the Government to take any legal steps they choose to enforce recovery of the money and we shall undergo all the sufferings that this may involve. We shall also allow our lands to be confiscated should they do so . . . .

*The 'assessment' was a tax paid by Indian farmers.

from Young India, *12 June 1918*

Source 3

Poster ordering a hartal *in 1917*

hartal protest strike, including the closing of all shops and businesses

BOYCOTT THE PRINCE'S VISIT.

CONGRESS . . . . ⎫
CENTRAL KHILAFAT ⎰ COMMITTEES' RESOLUTIONS
AND OUR DUTY

Do Not go to the Bunder
Do Not go to see the Procession
Do Not go to any Function held in connection with the visit
Do Not go to the Fete.
Do Not go to see the Illuminations
Do Not go to the Cricket Match
Do Not open Stalls in the Fair
Students should not take the sweets offered

BUT
OBSERVE **COMPLETE HARTAL** ON THE 17th
AND ATTEND

BONFIRE and PUBLIC MEETING
On the grounds near Elphinstone Mills at 10 a.m. in KHADI DRESS

Source 4

obstruction making things difficult
boycott avoiding, having no contact with

The Kaira satyagraha
The mainstay of the movement was a *pratidaya*, or sacred vow, which all were invited to take, whether able to pay or not, that they would not pay the revenue, and many copies of this were circulated in the villages and signatures obtained. Every method of *obstruction* was adopted; even the *boycott* of those who paid . . . . and Government servants engaged in the work of collection were subjected to all kinds of petty annoyance . . . . there were a few cases of forcible obstruction . . . but this was no part of Mr Gandhi's policy and his influence was strongly exercised on the side of peaceful methods.

from a report by the Collector of Kaira (i.e. the official who collected the assessment), 1917–18
Bombay Land Revenue Administration Report

Source 5

(Gandhi was accused of trying to excite disloyalty and opposition to the British Government)

(i) *Gandhi*: In my humble opinion, non-cooperation with evil is as much a duty as is cooperation with good. But in the past, non-cooperation has been deliberately expressed in violence to the evildoer. I am endeavouring to show my countrymen that violent non-cooperation only multiplies evil . . . . I am here, therefore, to invite and submit cheerfully to the highest penalty that can be inflicted upon me for what in law is a deliberate crime and what appears to me to be the highest duty of a citizen.

category type, sort
patriot a person devoted to his country

(ii) *The Judge, Mr C. N. Broomsfield, an Englishman*: . . . it will be impossible to ignore the fact that you are in a different *category* from any person I have ever tried or am likely to have to try. It would be impossible to ignore the fact that, in the eyes of millions of your countrymen, you are a great *patriot* and a great leader. Even those who differ from you in politics look upon you as a man of high ideals and of noble and of even saintly life. I have to deal with you in one character only. It is not my duty and I do not presume to judge or criticise you in any other character. It is my duty to judge you as a man subject to the law, who by his own admission has broken the law and committed what to an ordinary man must appear to be grave offence against the State. I do not forget that you have consistently preached against violence and that you have on many occasions, as I am willing to believe, done much to prevent violence.

from the Report of the trial of Gandhi, 18 March 1922

Source 6

What is worth learning from me is my love and not my strength to give a fight. My fighting strength is only a small fraction of my real life. And even that strength is the outcome of my truth, my sympathy, my love. All my fights, and fighting spirit, are worth nothing without that love.

from a speech made by Gandhi in Cutch, 1925

Source 7

infallible cannot fail

The march to Dandi
The non-violent method of action to bring about a change for the better was to Gandhi the only right method and, if rightly pursued, an *infallible* method. The great question was – how? How were we to begin? What form of civil disobedience should we take up that would be effective, suited to the circumstances, and popular with the masses? And then the Mahatma gave the hint. Salt* suddenly became a mysterious word, a word of power. The salt tax was to be attacked, the

Followers of Gandhi deliberately breaking the law by evaporating salt from sea water.

breach break
expedients methods, devices
efficacy effectiveness,
    success

salt laws were to be broken . . . . Then came the Dandi Salt March . . . . As people followed the fortunes of this marching column of *pilgrims* from day to day, the temperature of the country went up . . . . April came, and Gandhi drew near to the sea, and we waited for the word to begin civil disobedience by an attack on the salt laws. On 6 April Gandhi began the *breach* of the salt laws at Dandi beach and three or four days later permission was given to all Congress (Indian National Congress Party) organisations to do likewise and begin civil disobedience in their own areas . . . . All over the country salt manufacture was the topic of the day, and many curious *expedients* were adopted to produce salt . . . . As we saw the abounding enthusiasm of the people we felt ashamed of having questioned the *efficacy* of this method when it was first proposed by Gandhi. And we marvelled at the amazing knack of the man to impress the multitude and make it act in an organised way . . . .

*Salt was taxed by the British.

from the Autobiography *of J. Nehru (a friend of Gandhi and the first Prime Minister of independent India)*

Source 8
A cartoon from Punch, *1930*

Gandhi tells his genie, Nationalism, 'Remember – no violence.' The genie replies 'And what if I disobey *you*?' (Gandhi seems to be losing control of his movement.)

Questions

1   Use Sources 2, 3, 4 and 7 to explain, in your own words, the meaning of the term *satyagraha*. Give three examples of *satyagraha* in action.

2   Find as many statements as you can, in Sources 1–7, which show that violence was no part of Gandhi's plan for Indian freedom from the British Empire.

3   What evidence is there in Source 5 (ii) that even some of those opposed to Gandhi admired and respected his personality and methods?

4   Is Source 8 for or against Gandhi's civil disobedience campaign? Give reasons for your answer.

5   How would supporters of Gandhi defend their leader and his methods? Use the evidence provided to write a brief defence of his ideas and actions.

Case Study 2
A violent response – the problem of Palestine

Palestine is a small country, 150 miles long and seldom more than 30 miles wide. The Jews, or Hebrews, lived there off and on from the days of Abraham, but it was Moses, according to the Bible, who first told the Israelites that Palestine was the land promised them by God. The Jews inhabited Palestine until the first and second centuries AD during which most of them left following unsuccessful attempts to rid their homeland of Roman occupation forces.

In the seventh century AD, Arabs conquered Palestine and have been there ever since, living side by side with those Jewish people who had remained. Throughout history the Jews who had fled to other parts of the world had been persecuted and ill-treated. This led to the determination on the part of many Jewish people to return to their 'promised land' of Palestine. Some did go back, so that by 1914 there were 85 000 Jews in Palestine out of a total population of 700 000.

The fate of European Jews under Hitler brought worldwide support for the setting-up of a Jewish national home in Palestine. The Arabs in Palestine objected to this and violence broke out between Jews and Palestinians. The United Nations decided that Palestine should be divided into two states, one for the Jews and one for the Arabs. In 1948 the state of Israel was declared and was immediately attacked by other Arab countries who supported the Palestinians. Israel managed to win even more land than the UN had originally intended.

During the fighting about 600 000 Arabs fled their homes and went to other Arab countries, mainly Jordan. Since that first war, three more wars have taken place and more and more Palestinian Arabs have become refugees from their

Israel and her neighbours in the early 1980s.

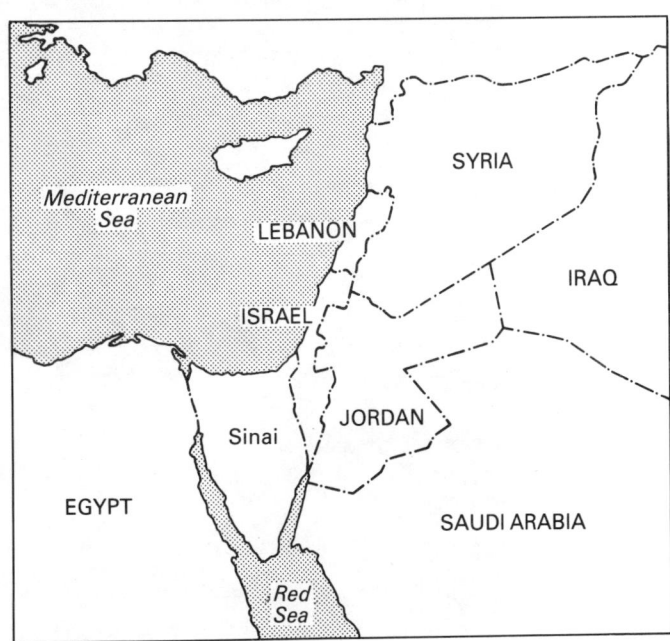

homeland. The Palestine Liberation Organisation was set up to demonstrate the bitterness of Palestinian Arabs both inside Israel and in refugee camps in other Arab countries.

In the years that followed, other Palestinian groups were formed, such as Black September and the Popular Front for the Liberation of Palestine. Terrorism was the chief method used by all these organisations to achieve their goals.

Source 1

Q. Our first question is when and how did the Palestine national liberation movement come about and how have its activities increased?
A. Our movement, the Palestine national liberation movement, El Fatah, was formed in 1956 . . . . Since then we, the Palestine people, have been thinking in terms of action and formed the Palestine national liberation movement. We trained youth and collected arms secretly until we set off our revolution on 1 January 1965 . . . .
Q. What are the political *objectives* of the Palestine national liberation movement, El Fatah – and is it possible to *define* the development of the movement as far it concerns the future of Palestine and in particular of the Jews in Palestine?
A. Our aim is to *liberate* our homeland, Palestine, from the Israeli occupation, ... and to establish an Arab Palestine State in which all religions *coexist*.

objectives aims
define explain
liberate free
coexist live together

Yasir Arafat, Chairman of the Palestine Liberation Organisation.

Q. What then are the means to attain these objectives?

A. We believe only in one means – the means of armed struggle in which we have full faith for the liberation of our country and the regaining of our land.

Q. Can you define the word *fedai* as it applies to the Palestine national liberation movement El Fatah?

A. Brother, *fedai* action is part of our armed revolution. This is the true meaning of the *fedai* action because it is part of the total revolution, no more and no less. Revolution means using arms, words, positive struggle, passive struggle, strikes, defiance such as that displayed by our people against the enemy occupiers – this is what revolution means. They include *fedai* operations by special units of our men against the enemy.

from an interview with Yasir Arafat, leader of El Fatah, 5 June 1968, on Radio Algiers

Source 2

inevitable cannot be avoided
rectify put right, correct
eliminates does away with, removes
material embarrassment shortage of weapons, soldiers, supplies
legends and epics stories of heroes, martyrs and people to look up to
liquidation destruction
mobilisation preparing armed forces for action

The role of the Palestinian resistance is, therefore, as follows:

1 To continue to strike during the period between the two battles – the battle of 5 June 1967, in which the Arab world was defeated, and the *inevitable* battle to *rectify* that defeat . . . .

2 The continuation of resistance has an important moral effect because it *eliminates* the fear which the Israeli enemy is trying to implant in the heart of the Arab fighter . . . .

3 Resistance is causing *material embarrassment* and psychological confusion to the enemy.

4 By strengthening its positions in the face of all the obstacles, the resistance may be able to play a major role in the battle with the enemy behind his lines when the decisive hour strikes.

5 Resistance, and this is the human aspect of its role, will symbolise the Palestinian element. Propaganda has tried to eliminate its existence, and even the feeling of its existence.

6 Finally, the resistance – particularly because of the enemy's overwhelming superiority – will by its courage and sacrifice give the Arab struggle its finest *legends and epics* . . .

This then, is the role of the resistance. It is one of the most splendid and noble roles, but not a decisive one. I mean that the resistance cannot achieve the *liquidation* of the Israeli aggression, which is a broader responsibility. It is the responsibility of the entire Arab nation on a broader and wider front, with complete concentration and *mobilisation* . . .

from H. Haykal, 'Death and Hope', Al-Ahram, 16 August 1968

Source 3

Extract from a report in The Times, *6 September 1972*

Israeli Olympic hostages all killed

All nine of the Israeli hostages seized by Arab guerrillas at the Olympic village in Munich yesterday, were killed early today during a gun battle between the terrorists and West German security forces at an airport near Munich.

Four of the guerrillas and a policeman died in the shooting at Furstenfeldbruck military airport where the Arabs were attempting to escape with their hostages.

A helicopter pilot was also reported to have been seriously wounded. A West German Government spokesman said that marksmen opened fire on the terrorists after helicopters carrying the Arabs and the hostages landed at the airport.

Because of the darkness, the security men did not hit all the Arabs and the terrorists then turned their weapons on the helicopters.

Herr Bruno Merck, the Bavarian Minister of the Interior, said that the wreckage of the helicopters was being searched in case some of the hostages had survived. He said one of the helicopters was blown up by a grenade.

Herr Hans Dietrich Genscher, the West German Federal Interior Minister, told a press conference this morning that he had offered himself as hostage to the Arabs when he went to negotiate with them at the Israel headquarters in the Olympic village yesterday. Early yesterday morning, the terrorists killed two Israelis when they occupied the team's headquarters.

Because of this, the Olympic Games were suspended.

The Arabs, members of the extremist Palestinian group Black September, threatened to kill their Israeli hostages if 200 Palestinian prisoners held in Israel were not released. Herr Brandt, the West German Chancellor, went to Munich to take charge of negotiations with the Arabs.

The Palestinians negotiate with the German Police Chief. Inside the building are Israeli Olympic athletes held as hostages.

Questions

6   (a) According to Yasir Arafat (Source 1), what are the main aims of El Fatah, the Palestine national liberation movement?
    (b) What methods are to be used in achieving this aim?

7   H. Haykal (Source 2) tells us that resistance has five main advantages. Explain these in your own words.

8   Source 3 is a front-page headline in one of the world's leading newspapers. How would this have helped the Palestinian cause?

9   What would Gandhi have thought of Palestinian methods? Explain in your own words using any of the sources at your disposal.

Case Study 3
Solidarity – Poland's free trade union

For several centuries, Poland has suffered at the hands of powerful neighbouring states which have succeeded in gaining control over all or part of the country. Only briefly, after the First World War, did the Polish people enjoy independence and freedom from foreign control. In September 1939 Poland was invaded by Hitler's armies and, yet again, Poles found themselves under foreign rule. However, as the Second World War drew to a close, the German forces were expelled from Poland by advancing Soviet armies.

Far from freeing the Poles, the USSR decided to draw an 'Iron Curtain' between Eastern Europe and Western Europe, and once more Poland fell under the influence of a foreign power. Although Poland is no longer permanently occupied by Soviet forces, the USSR still exercises control over Polish governments. Since 1945, Polish working people have on several occasions tried to show ruling communist governments that they would like changes in the way in which Poland is organised. In 1956, 1970 and 1976, serious riots and disturbances were met by force, often resulting in serious loss of life. Many Polish workers were particularly angry because they could not express their complaints through free trade unions. Instead they were 'represented' by the 'Polish United Workers' Party' which was completely under state control. By 1980 the situation had become very serious

The Gdansk shipyard where the Solidarity movement was born.

Source 1

indebtedness a country's debts to other countries
corruption rottenness, spoiled by selfishness and mistakes
activists people who took an active part

and a new development gave Polish people some hope for the future. It all began with a strike at a large shipyard in the Polish city of Gdansk.

(i) The situation in Poland was becoming worse and worse – there was the growing *indebtedness*, workers were being laid off, and in our bulletins we published information about government *corruption* long before it became public. We believed that the strike was bound to be successful if we organised it the right way, that it would be like an avalanche, because a lot of people were talking about these things. Also, I'd gone around my department, asking people questions about what they would do if there was a strike. The majority of people said, 'Of course, of course, if it's only touched, the whole avalanche will start.'

(ii) . . . . our first proposed date was Wednesday, 13 August. But we had to postpone it to the 14th because Walesa was not available, because he had to take care of his child that day. We needed the help of Lech Walesa. He was older than we were. We were only 23 years old. We had known Walesa for a long time because we were *activists* in the Free Trade Unions, and we had met him regularly. The whole shipyard knew him, not only the shipyard but the town. So the plan was to strike on the 14th. Walesa didn't even know up to the 13th when the strike would take place, because this was a secret. We had to be careful, because there were spies everywhere.

(iii) (Thursday 14th August 1980) At that moment, Lech Walesa, who entered the shipyard over the gate, appeared from behind the manager's shoulder. You could see he was very excited and he started to talk angrily.

Walesa asked the manager whether he recognised him – it was in a very aggressive way, and Gniech was simply astounded, he could barely speak, and so he said nothing. So Walesa said, 'Tell them why I was fired from the shipyard.' The manager was unable to say anything, and stood aside. I was the one writing the names down, of people elected to the strike committee, so I wrote Lech Walesa's name down, and I gave the list to him so that he could read it out. When Lech read out his own name, he asked if the people would accept him, whether he could stay on the strike committee even though he wasn't currently a worker in the shipyard. They accepted with enormous enthusiasm, because they knew him, because he had been working in the shipyard and from his activities in the Free Trade Unions.

from an interview with Jerzy Borowczak, a worker at the Lenin shipyard in Gdansk

Lech Walesa – the leader of Solidarity.

Source 2

strike bulletin the news-sheet of the striking workers
logo sign, symbol, design
throngs crowds

I started to think of a slogan. There were so many on the walls . . . The word 'solidarity' kept recurring in them. It was also the title of the *strike bulletin*. I chose the word because, in the strongest way, it emphasised what was happening among the people.

I don't recall exactly when the form of the *logo* came to my mind, you know how in a tightly-packed crowd people lean on each other? This was the character of the *throngs* at the shipyard gate. The people standing there didn't crowd together, pushing and shoving, but they supported each other. In the same way, the letters of the word should support one another . . . . I was shocked at how widespread my design became: on the lapel of Walesa's jacket, on the street and on television and in the daily press. What an impact it has had in the memory, on the imagination, of all Poles.

The testimony of Jerzy Janiszewski, a student in Gdansk during the strike

The famous Solidarity logo carried by supporters of the banned trade union in 1987.

Source 3

humanitarian concerned with the rights of ordinary people
mere pittance small amount of money
disrupt cause to fail, break up

(i) *20 August 1980*
Our strike enjoys the support and sympathy of the entire country and of other countries in the world, because our 21 demands are deeply *humanitarian*. The strikers and society at large are well aware of this and it is a source of our strength. The workers are not fighting for a *mere pittance* for themselves but 'For justice for the whole nation'. We have to oppose the local authorities' attempts to *disrupt* the unity of our strike movement. We live up to the words: 'Man is born free'.

(ii) *28 August 1980*
We are the true representatives of the coastal workers, and we think that the workers of the whole country share our views. We are ready to discuss all problems and to ensure all our responsibilities in undertaking joint actions. But we can do this only if we have the confidence of the workers, a confidence that the present trade unions have lost.

from Solidarity Strike Bulletin *(the strikers' own newspaper, printed in Gdansk shipyard)*

Source 4

free association right to organise together in unions
political prisoners people in prison because of their political beliefs

The workers' demands
Solidarity put forward twenty-one demands, amongst which the ones below were of major importance:

(i) free trade unions – 'amongst basic human rights is the right of workers to *free association* in unions which genuinely represent them'.
(ii) The right to strike.
(iii) Freedom of expression – their own newspapers and the right to print what they wished in them 'whether or not this suits the authorities'.
(iv) Release of *political prisoners*.
(v) Economic reform – 'definite steps be taken to lead the country out of its present (economic) crisis.'
(N.B. Poland's debt to other countries was, in 1975, $8000 million. By 1979 this had become $20 000 million.)
(vi) 'Positive selection – people in leading positions should be chosen on the basis of qualifications rather than (Communist) party membership'.
(vii) Welfare – improvements in working conditions, retirement pensions, maternity leave, housing waiting-lists, etc.

Adapted from The Birth of Solidarity *(translated and introduced by A. Kemp-Welch, Macmillan/ St Antony's College, Oxford, 1983)*

Source 5

provocations causes of
violence

(*The strike at the Gdansk shipyard lasted eighteen days.*)
We issued permits for food shops to reopen. Delivery lorries still operated, so too
did the bakeries. The canning factory stayed at work so that the fish would not be
wasted. The factory that made tins had to work as well, as did the transport.
Drivers wore red and white arm-bands and flags were flown outside the shops.
We used our influence to stop the sale of alcohol, in order to prevent *provocations*. Even the sale of beer was prohibited. All this was directed by the
eighteen-member Strike Committee, consisting principally of workers.
*from the memoirs of Anna Walentynowicz, a crane driver and a founder-member of Solidarity
(Warsaw, 1981)*

Source 6

mass media TV, radio,
newspapers, etc.
reinstated given back their
jobs

(*The agreement between Solidarity and the Polish Government is long and
detailed. Below is a brief summary of the main points.*)
- (i)   It is necessary to form new, self-governing trade unions as real
representatives of the working class.
- (ii)   . . . the government will guarantee and ensure full respect for the
independence and self-government of the new trade unions.
- (iii) The right to strike will be guaranteed by the law on trade unions now
in preparation.
- (iv)   The new trade unions should have a genuine opportunity to express
their opinion in public on the major decisions which determine the
living standards of working people.
- (v)   Broadcasting, the press and publishing should express a wide variety of
ideas and opinions. Religious groups should be given access to *the
mass media*. There will be complete observance of freedom of expression and opinion in public and professional life.
- (vi)   Workers and students unjustly dismissed during the strikes of 1970
and 1976 will be *reinstated*.
- (vii) Economic reform will be speeded up and will involve representatives of
trade unions. Information on social and economic reform will be made
available to the general public.
- (viii) The wages of all groups of employees will gradually be raised, above
all those of the lowest paid.
- (ix)   . . . people in leading positions will be selected on the basis of
qualifications and ability . . . .
- (x)   A wide range of welfare improvements will be introduced, dealing with
health, working conditions, pensions, family allowances, etc.

The Gdansk Agreement – adapted from The Birth of Solidarity, *A. Kemp-Welch,
St Antony's/Macmillan, 1983)*

Source 7

Dear friends! We go back to work on September 1. We all know what this day
reminds us of. What we are thinking about on that day. About our motherland,
about the national cause, about the common interests of the family whose name is
Poland. We have been thinking a lot about this during the strike. That's what we
are thinking about as we end this strike.

  Have we achieved everything we wanted, everything we desired, all that we are
dreaming of? I always say frankly and openly what I think. So now I will say
frankly: not everything, but we all know that we've achieved a lot. You've trusted
me all this time, so believe what I'm telling you. We have achieved all that in the
present situation we could achieve. We'll achieve the rest too because we have the
most important thing: our independent, self-governing trade unions. This is our
guarantee for the future.

Lech Walesa declares the strike ended – The Solidarity Sourcebook *(New Star Books, 1982)*

Questions

13   (a) What were the main complaints of the workers in the shipyards at Gdansk
against the Polish Government? (Sources 1, 3, 4.)
      (b) Which of these complaints seem to you to be greater than *just* ordinary trade

union demands (e.g. better pay; shorter working-hours; improved working conditions; etc)?

14 Look up the meaning of the word 'solidarity' in a dictionary. Does its meaning appear to you to describe the activities of the striking workers at Gdansk?

15 What evidence is there in Source 5 that Solidarity began, in Gdansk, to take over the job of running the city?

16 According to Sources 6 and 7, how successful was Solidarity?

17 (a) Use the table below to briefly summarise the methods of resistance you have investigated in this exercise.

Leader	Type of resistance	Method(s)
(Example) Gandhi	Non-violent. Peaceful non-cooperation and civil disobedience.	Refusing to pay taxes. Boycotts. Marches. Obstruction.

(b) Construct a second chart, table or diagram of your own to show the advantages and disadvantages of each method of resistance as you see them.

18 Can you think of any other types of resistance practised in the world today? If so, give brief details.

8 Undertaking a personal investigation of a twentieth-century Issue

Introduction

It can be a very rewarding experience indeed to produce something which is largely the result of your own efforts and abilities. This is particularly true when someone else recognises the value and orginality of your achievement and tells you so! The main reward is knowing that a task has been well done and so any assessment of that task should be based upon *the way you set about it* as much as the end-product. We call the way you set about a task, 'the process'. You should then, be assessed on the process *and* the product.

More frequently these days, and particularly with the introduction of GCSE courses into schools, you are being asked to produce coursework which contributes towards your final achievement. The object of this exercise is to encourage you to think about a *personal investigation* of a historical problem or issue connected with the course you are undertaking.

Before you begin this enquiry, it would be a good idea to choose a problem or issue which interests you so that you can carry out the methods and processes of investigation. This will require some thought and some discussion with your teacher.

Selecting a problem or issue

The selection of coursework is sometimes left to teachers but often students are given some choice in what they wish to investigate. However the enquiry is chosen, it should usually take the form of *a problem which requires investigation*.

This is because there is very little point in undertaking a study of a topic which does not allow you to use your findings to reach a conclusion.

Task (1)

Knowing little if anything about the history of China in the twentieth century, you might be able to work in pairs or groups to decide which of the following would make the best choice for an investigation.
(a) China 1919 to 1949.
(b) The Communists in China – 1919 to 1949.
(c) Why and how did the Communists succeed in taking power in China by 1949?

Before you make your choice, ask the following questions about each of the proposed enquiries:
(i) Does it encourage you to make decisions or reach conclusions?
(ii) Does it give you a clear idea of exactly what you are going to investigate?
(iii) Could you *use* your findings or do you simply have to locate information and then rewrite it in your own words?
(iv) Is it manageable? (Would it enable you to limit your researches to a sensible level, or could you go on researching such an enquiry without any clear restrictions on its length or scope?)
Once you have decided which of the three enquiries is the most suitable for you, you should be prepared to defend your decision by referring to the four questions.

Choosing a problem or issue for investigation is one of the most vital stages of such work. The next, equally important step is the organising of your enquiry.

The nine question steps

(From Schools Council Curriculum Bulletin 9, 'Information Skills in the Secondary Curriculum')

1	What do I need to do?	PLANNING
2	Where could I go?	RESEARCHING
3	How do I get to the information?	
4	Which resources shall I use?	
5	How shall I use the resources?	
6	What should I make a record of?	
7	Have I got the information I need?	
8	How should I present it?	PRESENTING
9	What have I achieved?	ASSESSING

We live in a world in which information is increasingly available on a vast range of subjects and in a wide variety of media. It is very easy to become submerged in facts and details, and so it is important to learn to manage information. This means *careful planning* to obtain the information *you* want, the sources relevant to *your* enquiry.

You should begin to look upon your personal investigation as a campaign or series of tasks which all enable you to succeed in your chosen course of action. In this case, as the chart above shows, there are four stages to your campaign. These are:

> Planning
> Researching
> Presenting
> Assessing

Your plan of campaign (What do I need to do?)
The first thing you need to do is to acquaint yourself with the background to the problem or issue you have chosen. You can do this by reading a section of a book, watching a TV programme, or simply talking to someone who may know something about the issue. At this stage you do not need to record your findings or undertake any deep investigations.

Having gained a general view of the problem, you should then produce a list of questions or statements which will give you a detailed plan of how you expect to investigate and structure your study. An example of such a plan is shown below. You must remember that plans rarely remain unchanged for long! You may, in the course of your enquiries, add to or subtract from your original plan. You may have omitted an important line of investigation or you could find that one or two parts of the plan are not really relevant. (You would benefit from keeping all versions of your planning in order to show that you have been thinking and adapting your ideas.)

An example of a plan of campaign – Stage 1

Name:	Debbie Symonds
Topic:	The Communist victory in China.
Enquiry:	Why were the Communists able to gain control in China in 1949?
Length:	1500 words.

Plan of campaign
The investigation will examine the reasons for the increase in support for the Communists between 1921 and 1949 and the factors which enabled them to set up the People's Republic on 1 October 1949. It is not intended to examine in detail the general political problems before 1921 except where these are obviously linked to the investigation.

1   Why and how did the Chinese Communist Party (CCP) come into being in 1921?

2   From which sections of Chinese society did support come for the CCP and

how far did this support increase between 1921 and 1929?

3   Why did the CCP cooperate with Sun Yat-Sen's party, the Kuomintang, (KMT) until 1927? What brought this cooperation to an end?

4   What actions were taken by the new KMT leader, Chiang Kai-shek and his followers, which threatened the existence of the CCP between 1927 and 1934?

5   What was the importance of the Long March to the survival of the CCP and the leadership of Mao Tse-tung?

6   How did the threat from Japan between 1936 and 1945 help Mao and the CCP against Chiang Kai-shek?

7   What factors enabled the Communists to defeat the nationalists between 1946 and 1949?
    I will consider: – the role of Mao Tse-tung.
                     – the superior leadership of the communist forces.
                     – the support of most peasants for the Communists.
                     – the lack of morale amongst KMT troops.
                     – the superior organisation of the Communist forces.

8   Resources to be used:
    Books: C. K. Macdonald, *Modern China*.
           N. Tarling, *Mao and the Transformation of China*.
           Schools Council History Project, *The Rise of Communist China*.

You will note that this is Stage 1 of Debbie's plan of campaign. She expects to make changes as her investigation proceeds. She had included a basic list of resources with which to begin her enquiries, but again, she knows that she will have to add to this list.

Task (2)

You should now have a good idea of the first two stages of planning a personal investigation:

    (i) choosing a problem to investigate;
    (ii) planning your investigation.

Now proceed to carry out these tasks in an enquiry of your own. (*NB* It may be that your teacher decided to select the problem or issue for you. If this is so, proceed to stage ii.)

Remember that you cannot successfully plan your study without *some* background knowledge of the problem. You should do some general reading first unless you have covered the topic already and know something about it.

Researching your project

'Research' is a word you will meet often these days. At the end of a film or television programme you will see a list of credits which will include cameramen, producer, director and frequently now, 'Research by . . .'. What is meant here is that the material upon which the film or programme was based has been 'discovered' by this researcher, who has consulted various books, sought information by personal interview, and so on.

The meaning of the word 'research' changes according to the level at which the 'discovering' is being attempted. For example, you may have undertaken a project in junior or middle school for which you were only required to look at one or two books. On the highest level, professional historians carry out investigations by examining *all* the available sources of information (or evidence) on a given topic or happening.

It is not expected that you should be as thorough as the professionals! However, you must be aware that research is '*careful search or enquiry; scientific study or investigation to discover facts*'. There is nothing haphazard or vague about research. It must be:

    (a) *methodical*   organised to ensure maximum returns for your efforts.

(b) *specific*	concerned with your area of interest only. It is important to beware of being sidetracked into facts, issues or ideas that have no relation to the enquiry you are making.
(c) *accurate*	findings from whatever sources should be summarised correctly for your use so that factual errors or incorrect reporting of opinions, ideas or issues are avoided.
(d) *comprehensive*	involving an investigation of as wide a range of historical materials as time and availability will allow.

Thus it is insufficient merely to base your researches on one or two sources. Neither is it wise to rely upon one *type* of source.

Some useful hints on research work

1 Try to do some *general reading* on the topic you have chosen, to get an impression of the overall scope of your subject, the main issues involved and the most important facts. You may find some interesting leads and perhaps uncover varying opinions.

2 Compile a *resource list* which contains references to the sources you intend to use. This should not be a static list, i.e. a 'once-and-for-all', final statement of sources. You may wish to add to the list or even to disregard materials which are not useful. *NB* It is essential that you use one source to give you leads to others. Most history books, for example, contain bibliographies (booklists for further reading, often with details of usefulness).

3 Wherever possible, include *primary sources* in your researches. Remember that these are the raw materials of history and will enable you to form views without being influenced by the ideas of historians (though you should not, of course, ignore secondary interpretations). There are some useful collections of documents, either on particular topics (e.g. Jackdaw folders and the Archive Series, often available in schools), or on a particular period (e.g. *They Saw it Happen 1897–1940* and *Documents on World History, 1919 to the Present*.) Extracts from primary sources may also appear in secondary evidence. For example a film made recently on a twentieth-century topic may well contain 'live footage' (i.e. snips of film from the actual time).

4 *Visual sources* come in a variety of forms and it is important that you do not see these as being merely decorative or ornamental. You can draw your own views using pictures, maps, graphs, photographs, film, etc. You must get into the habit of investigating visual sources as thoroughly as you would examine a document or book. Most of these sources will repay careful and detailed examination and will suggest other questions and directions for study. No one undertaking a social topic (that is, one concerned with the way in which people lived, their conditions, etc.), can possibly give a full view without using visual evidence.

Task (3)   Using your visual sources

As with the first task you were asked to do, this one requires no knowledge about Chinese history. The comments you are asked to make are *general* and you need only refer to the sources below.

Using visual evidence is very much like using any other kind of source material – to get the best out of it you need to *ask the right questions*. Two of the three visual sources below are accompanied by questions which should help you to gain useful information and impressions. Your task is to investigate the two visuals by answering the questions and then to invent questions of your own relating to the third source.

Source 1

Chinese postage stamps
The stamp on the left shows the nationalist (i.e. anti-Communist) leader, Chiang Kai-shek (1945); the one on the right shows the Communist leader, Mao Tse-Tung (1950).

Questions

(a) Describe the flags of the opposing sides.
(b) What impression do you get of the two rival leaders from their pictures?
(c) What evidence is there that Mao wanted to show the power of Communist China?
(d) Would you say these stamps had some propaganda value? Why?

Source 2

A map of China showing how the Communists gained control of China between 1947 and 1949

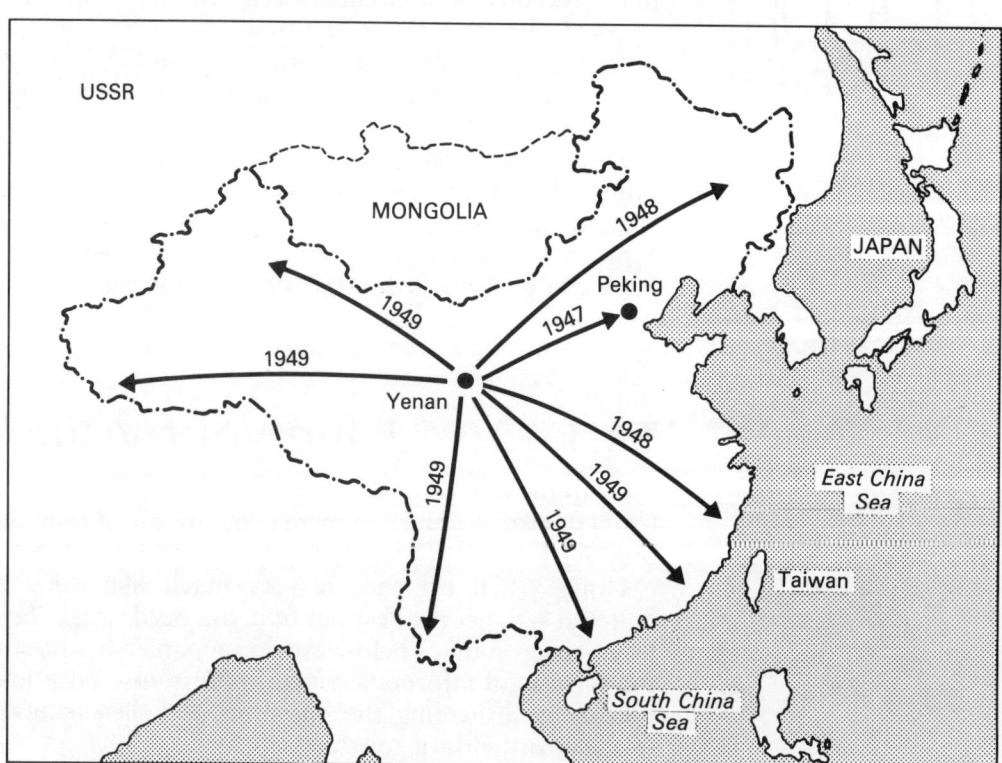

Questions

(a) From which stronghold did the Chinese Communist Party launch its attempt to gain control of the country?

(b) According to the map which parts of China were the most important to the CCP?

(c) How *useful* is this map as a source of information for the victory of the CCP in China?

Source 3
A painting showing communist fighters on the Long March to escape from their nationalist enemies (NB This is a *secondary* source painted over 30 years after the event).

Finding resources
The obvious place to start is in asking, Where can I find material that would help me investigate the problem I have selected?' Let's start in school.

(i) *The classroom* Your teacher will have access to a variety of sources which she/he may well advise you to consider. Ordinary textbooks may give you a springboard from which to launch your enquiry. More detailed books may also be recommended and your teacher will know roughly what is available. These books will often contain *bibliographies* (lists of books for further reference), which will quickly sum up other useful sources available on a subject.

(ii) *The school and local libraries* Almost all libraries work on the same system, called the *Dewey system*. This means that once you find out how to use the school library you should be able to use any library. If you use the Dewey classification you might, researching for example South Africa, look up a number of phrases or words: (e.g. South African History; British Empire; Apartheid; Racism: Boer; etc.). Each of these words would give you a number, for example 945.2. If you can find the shelves with books numbered from 900 to 99, you should be able find what is available for your enquiry. However, each of the headings mentioned may have a different number and you must be careful to investigate as many possibilities as you think necessary. Thoroughness is essential!

(iii) *Visual resources* For a project on the twentieth century you will probably be aware that a lot of newsreel and photographic evidence exists. In school you may have lists of television programmes, tape/slide programmes and tape-recordings you could use. Look through the lists of what is available and see if anything looks useful. Libraries occasionally keep books of photographs, newspapers and magazines. You might be able to borrow, photocopy or sketch pictures from these sources. For example you might be working on the German invasion of the

Rhineland in 1936. If you know when the event occurred you might be able to consult *The Times* or *Punch* magazine for that date and find out how the British reacted. You could find a cartoon which you could photocopy and paste into your project.

(iv) *Family, relatives, friends, contacts* You might be researching the General Strike, the Suez Crisis or the British escape from Dunkirk in 1940. Ask around! There could well be someone in your neighbourhood, or even in your family, who was there or remembers the event. You could interview them. A tape-recorder would obviously be helpful here.

(v) *Other sources* A whole variety of personal ideas could be exploited. Here are just a few that previous students have tried:

- *Keesing's Archives*, available in libraries, provide a wide variety of contemporary sources for your research.
- *Pressure groups*, using people such as Amnesty International or Greenpeace. (Addresses available from the local library).
- *Government departments* may provide useful information sheets. Even your local MP might be able to help, depending on your topic.
- *Document collections* might add a significant number of primary sources to your resource list. The most famous of these are the Jackdaw series, but there are others.
- *Foreign embassies* are often willing to provide fact sheets and propaganda material. Obvious care is needed in the use of such sources, but they are worth studying to obtain one point of view.

Task (4)

Use the chart below to help you draw up a research programme. Take a copy of the chart to your school library, your local library, to the school resources centre or audio-visual area if there is one.

Personal Investigation – Record of Resources

Name .... *Topic* ....

Nature of investigation ....

....

....

Resource List

Item	Type	Located	Ref.(s)
The Heart of the Dragon BBC	TV Programme	Audio-visual Room	Prog. 2
Modern China, G. K. Macdonald	Book	School Library	Pages 14–34
The Rise of Communist China	Tape/ Filmstrip	Hist. Dept	Side 2
China since 1949	Radio (Radio History 14–16, BBC)	Hist. Dept	Prog. 1

You might decide to add extra columns to your chart showing, for example, the date you obtained the item and how useful it was. When you finally come to report your findings after you have completed all your researching you should use the chart to write an introduction which tells your teacher the problems you faced, the resources you found most useful, the weaknesses of some sources, and so on. Alternatively, you could use the chart to give your teacher an oral account of these things.

Presenting your project

The skills of planning, investigation, analysis and evaluation will count for very little unless you are able to *communicate* your findings to your readers. Obviously they are more likely to be impressed by a project which is neat, well laid-out, and relevantly illustrated, than one which is shoddy, scrappy and contains a minimum of visuals.

The first priority should be to ensure that your written account is clear, legible and coherent. Sentences should be written in good English and care should be taken to avoid errors in grammar, expression and spelling, which convey a bad impression. You should use your own words at all times and you should try to avoid irrelevant details which make little or no contribution to your argument or analysis.

Many students find it helpful to organise their essay under headings and sub-headings. This helps you to keep your mind on a particular stage of your argument and to present a logical, organised response. It may also help you to distinguish between the most important points you wish to make and those which may be relevant but less significant. You may choose to take your headings and sub-headings from your plan of campaign.

Wherever possible you should try to include relevant diagrams, pictures, maps, graphs and charts. *Use them.* Label them carefully and refer to them in your written text. Investigate them as carefully as you would written sources. Point out contradictions they may suggest, or how they confirm your written sources. Try to be imaginative in the way you present information. A visual medium can make the same point as a list of figures or statistics, and a colourful graph, pictogram or pie-chart might be much more stimulating.

An assessor will be impressed by a project which is evidently well organised. Consider the advantages of using a contents list and/or an index. If you use headings and sub-headings make sure they stand out. Use *space* effectively so that your project does not appear to be cramped and badly laid-out. First impressions *are* important! Try to make an immediate visual impact.

Summary Presentation – 'Dos' and 'Do nots'

Do . . .	Do not . . .
1 *Use headings* where possible to indicate areas of importance in your study. This should help you to organise your findings in a logical fashion. 2 *Use visual aids* to present your findings where appropriate. (Maps, graphs, diagrams, even useful photocopied visual evidence.)	1 *Write up your findings in note form.* (You should use proper English sentences and paragraphs.) 2 *Copy extracts* or unacknowledged quotations straight from your sources. 3 *Allow yourself to be sidetracked* from the main thread of your study. Irrelevant details or ideas will only

unabridged unshortened,
unabbreviated, uncut

3 Try to be *original* in the way you present your work. Create your own mode of presentation if at all possible. Try to transcribe appropriate evidence into an attractive (possibly visual) mode.
4 *Use your plan of procedure.* The reporting of your findings *must* follow your final draft plan of campaign. Part of the object of the exercise is to plan carefully and then to follow your plan.

confuse the issues and waste your time.
4 *Include long, unabridged supportive 'aids'* in the main narrative. (Timelines, extracts from Acts of Parliament, relevant newspaper reports, etc., should be included as appendixes.)
5 *Repeat or duplicate information or ideas.* Be concise where possible.

Recording your progress

Undertaking a personal investigation requires a completely different attitude from work which is set by your teacher for everyone in your group. When you take on a project like this, *you* supply the initiative, the imagination, the determination, the organisation and, if you really want to make a good job of it, *you* must contribute to the assessment of your study!

Your teacher will give you advice, guidance and suggestions – but the onus is upon you to assess your own progress. Most students find that it is helpful to keep a diary which records their progress through a personal study. In this diary they make a note of what they do on any particular day, what they discover which is new to them, suggestions for further enquiries, problems they encounter, etc. (In fact, it is useful to follow the 'Nine Question Steps' mentioned earlier.) You might also include in your diary details of timings, showing what proportion of time you allocated to planning, to research and to reporting your findings. Your diary could then be submitted with your finished study.

Using your completed study, your Record of Resources sheet and your diary, you should be able, with your teacher, to work out what you have achieved. You may find the Self-Assessment exercise on the next page useful.

Personal Investigation   *My Record of Progress*
Name _____ Class/Group _____
Problem for investigation _____
_____
_____

Date submitted for assessment _____

1   Why did you choose this *particular* problem for investigation?

2   How did you begin your investigation?
    (a) Where did you go?

    (b) Were you able to obtain useful resources? Explain.

    (c) Which resources did you find most useful and why?

3   Did you have to make any changes to your first Plan of Campaign?
    If so, what were they and why did you make these changes?

4   Now that you have finished your investigation, do you think
    your *final* plan was the most useful one for you? Explain why/why not.

5   What problems did you encounter during the course of your investigations?
    How did you overcome them?

6   How do you rate the way in which you planned and organised your
    investigation? (Tick boxes).

Well planned and organised	Most of it was well-planned	Rather disorganised. Could do better	Totally disorganised

7   How do you rate the way in which you researched your investigation? (Tick boxes).

Thorough research using a wide range of resources	Used only few resources but used them well	Relied upon one or two resources and could have looked further	Very little research attempted

8   How do you rate the way in which you presented your investigation? (Tick boxes).

Neat, clear, well laid out, good visuals	Presentable. Could have used more imagination	Rather untidy and few visuals used	Looks very messy

9   If you were to undertake a similar investigation in the future, what changes
    would you make to improve your technique and your finished product?

Signed   Signed
(Student) _____   (Tutor) _____
                                                    Date _____

Unit Title		Attitudes		Skills	
The sinking of the Lusitania		Shows a willingness to consider an issue from different points of view and to appreciate the difficulty of making 'accurate' judgements.		Can comprehend, analyse, interpret and evaluate a range of historical sources. Can support conclusions with evidence.	
The Jarrow Crusade		Is willing to explore the values and motives of a group in their historical context. Is able to compare and contrast this context to his/her own.		Can use historical sources to investigate and to analyse the motives of a group of people.	
The destruction of Guernica		Demonstrates a readiness to consider a historical problem from two sides and to make decisions based on the objective consideration of evidence.		Is able to use evidence to explain two sides of an argument. Can evaluate sources to show where bias and distortion might be present.	
The assassination of Trotsky		Shows an interest in an historical character from the point of view of motives, actions and the consequences of his or her activities.		Is able to consider a variety of explanations for an historical incident and to select the most likely one and support the choice by using evidence.	
Propaganda – 'the war that Hitler won'?		Is willing to investigate visual and other sources with the same critical curiosity as written evidence.		Can recognise different types of propaganda and can identify some of the advantages of each type.	
The Cuba crisis		Shows a readiness to put aside preconceived notions of 'good' and 'bad' in considering an important East/West dispute.		Is able to use evidence to appreciate both sides of an argument and to point out the strengths and weaknesses of the stances taken by the disputing parties.	
Reactions to opression		Accepts that historical people react to problems in different ways or is willing to contribute to discussion about the validity and effectiveness of the different methods.		Is able to make accurate and appropriate comparisons by careful consideration of evidence.	
Undertaking a personal investigation		Shows initiative in selecting planning and researching an investigation.		Is able to make an effective plan of procedure that works. Can locate and use a range of sources. Can present findings in an appropriate manner.	

	Concepts		Imagination		Vocabulary
	Is able to exploit the sources provided to speculate and hypothesise on relative responsibility for a historical incident.		Can use sources and imagination to defend a point of view. Can imaginatively represent the views of people of another time and place.		Is able to use appropriate key terms necessary to defend a judgement on a controversial issue.
	Can understand that there have been and continue to be areas of economic and social depression and is able to explain some of the causes and effects of these forces.		Can use sources and statistics to imaginatively reconstruct and comment upon the lifestyle and standards of living of the people under study.		Can understand and accurately use appropriate economic terms associated with the problem, such as 'depression', 'boom', 'decline', etc.
	Is able to comprehend the importance of public opinion and world opinion in allocating responsibility for a tragic incident.		Can exploit sources imaginatively to produce an argument which shows clearly the perspective of one side in a dispute.		Is able to use the correct terms to identify the participants in the Civil War.
	Demonstrates an understanding of the role of individuals in a specific historical incident.		Is able to write a newspaper report to reflect imaginatively the views of one of the key individuals in the particular situation.		Accurately uses key words and terms in supporting the decisions taken about the likely explanation of the incident.
	Is able to show a basic appreciation of the influence exerted by the mass media over the minds and hearts of people on a given historical context.		Can apply general characteristics of Nazi propaganda to hypothetical situations in an imaginative way.		Understands and identifies the language and symbolism of propaganda. Is able to appreciate that slogan and symbolism have advantages in propaganda.
	Understands that the security of the world is very much dependent upon the relations between the superpowers.		Imaginatively renders the strengths and weaknesses in the cases of both sides in the dispute by using evidence and avoiding preconceived notions.		Is able to deploy some of the basic vocabulary of confrontation and to use correct words and terms in attacking or defending the counter-arguments.
	Is able to understand a variety of interpretations of the idea of 'oppression'.		Can use imagination to view reactions of historical people in their context. Can imaginatively cross-reference between case-studies.		Uses technical terms related to individual case studies accurately and appropriately.
	Can understand the various elements of the research process and apply them in practice.		Can use imagination in formulating a problem for investigation. Can present the results of findings in an imaginative way.		Can locate the meanings of words, phrases and terms encountered in the course of investigation.